HOME *Fronts*

NEW AMERICANISTS

A series edited by Donald E. Pease

HOME
Fronts

Domesticity and Its Critics in the

Antebellum United States

LORA ROMERO

Duke University Press

Durham and London

1997

© 1997 Duke University Press

All rights reserved   Printed in the

United States of America on acid-free paper ∞

Typeset in Perpetua by Keystone Typesetting, Inc.

Library of Congress Cataloging-in-Publication Data

appear on the last printed page of this book.

❧ CONTENTS

❧ PREFACE

In the process of writing this book, I came to dread the casual query: "What is your book about?" For interlocutors who obviously did not desire a prospectus-length description of materials and method, "the cultural politics of nineteenth-century domesticity" seemed like the most handy response. But I soon discovered that this response produced more confusion than enlightenment; it seemed to lead to the mistaken impression that *Home Fronts* addressed only women writers and that it took the polemical form of either condemnation or celebration.

Readers may also bring similar expectations to this book. Although *Home Fronts* gives considerable attention to women's literary expression, it reads the work of male writers usually considered critics of domesticity as agents in creating what they denounced. Furthermore, I dispense with the familiar polemics of twentieth-century literary criticism by arguing that domesticity was neither simply conservative nor simply subversive. Without sacrificing inquiry into cultural politics, I insist upon the plurality of political positions that representations of middle-class home life supported in the antebellum period, and I stress the dependency of their political significance upon the different communities, populations, and institutions in the context of which they were deployed.

Domesticity's own gendered tropes of domination and resistance determine the bifurcated evaluations characterizing contemporary critical discussion of antebellum culture. The gender binarism through which domesticity organized its representations of domination and resistance has helped sustain critical efforts to imagine cultural spaces liberated from the infection of power relations. We have returned to domesticity over and again because the dyadic model of domination and resistance generated through the language of separate spheres supports the concept of high authorial consciousness—the modern concept that we use to impart value to both canonical and noncanonical works. Hence *Home Fronts* is as much about contemporary critical investments in domesticity as it is about domesticity itself.

My personal investment in domesticity as a topic undoubtedly reflects my own experiences of dislocation as I wrote this book. The substance of *Home Fronts* was written in three different states while I was associated with three different universities. Although these relocations prolonged the process of writing, thinking about the friends and colleagues I found in all these places who contributed so liberally to this book and who made me feel at home prevents me from regretting my peripatetic existence.

My oldest debts go back to graduate school—to Eric Sundquist, Michael Rogin, and Walter Michaels, the readers of a Ph.D. dissertation in which some of the chapters that follow found rudimentary expression. I thank them for the labor and care they as readers gave my fledgling work. But I also thank them for being engaging teachers and critics who stimulated my initial interest in the period and the critical issues that have continued to nourish my work.

Postdoctoral fellowships I received from the Ford Foundation and the University of Texas at Austin in 1990–1991 gave me the break from teaching that I needed to begin to reconstruct my interest into the project that eventuated in this book. Ann Cvetkovich, Lynn Wardley, and Jeff Nunokawa played crucial roles in this process by listening to my ideas, advising me on drafts, and provoking me into new ways of thinking both in conversations and through their writings. Many other colleagues and friends also provided me with a sense of intellectual community as challenging as much as it was encouraging. Of these I would especially like to acknowledge Diana Fuss, Emory Elliott, Ramón Saldívar, Evan Carton, Barbara Harlow, Margit Stange, Gretchen Ritter, Lisa Moore, Ann Norton, Rita Copeland, Jackie Henkel, and Shirley Samuels. Over the years, Myra Hindus supported me through less scholarly but no less important means: understanding, encouragement, and fun.

In their official capacities as readers of the manuscript of this book or of articles on which chapters are based, Wai-Chee Dimock, Walt Herbert, and an anonymous Duke reader suggested revisions from which this book has benefitted. Thanks to Kenneth Kidd, Chiyuma Elliot, Lisa Lenker, and John González for their indispensable research assistance, some of which a Coghlan Faculty Fellowship from Stanford University helped finance.

All of the brief expressions of appreciation I've given thus far seem insufficient, but brief acknowledgments seem especially inadequate for three friends in particular—Dana Nelson, Cathy Davidson, and Ken Wissoker. Their intellectual generosity, overwhelming kindness, and remarkable tact got me through the bleakest days of writing. Gratitude, however, explains only the smallest part of the enormous respect and affection I feel for them.

Finally, I am grateful to the following journals and editors for granting permission to use previously published articles and essays on which some chapters are based: chapter 1 draws upon an essay appearing in *The Columbia History of the American Novel,* ed. Emory Elliott (New York: Columbia University Press, 1991); chapter 2 was published in *American Literature* 63 (1991) and subsequently reprinted in *The Culture of Sentiment: Race, Gender, and Sentimentality in 19th-Century America,* ed. Shirley Samuels (New York: Oxford University Press, 1992) and in *Subjects & Citizens: Nation, Race, & Gender from Oroonoko to Anita Hill,* ed. Cathy N. Davidson and Michael Moon (Durham: Duke University Press, 1995); a version of chapter 4 appeared in *American Literary History* 1 (winter 1989) and was reprinted in *The American Literary History Reader,* ed. Gordon Hutner (New York: Oxford University Press, 1995).

This book arises out of the intersection of two kinds of concerns: one, a literary-archival fascination with the still understudied historical and cultural materials of mid-nineteenth-century domesticity; the other, a theoretical preoccupation with cultural politics. Studying the history of domesticity (constituted by, as I will later argue, its proponents and practitioners as much as its detractors and evaders) suggested to me that the available paradigms for thinking about mid-nineteenth-century culture were insufficiently interpretive, being themselves unable to represent power—and resistance to it—in a manner fundamentally different from that informing the materials and practices under consideration.

This limitation was particularly troublesome given the subject of my study; one cannot engage the topic of domesticity or its cultural and institutional offspring without, at the very least, implicitly addressing theories of hegemony and resistance. Since at least the publication of Herman Melville's famous review of Nathaniel Hawthorne's *Twice-Told Tales*, cultural authorities have depended upon the nineteenth-century middle-class home in order to calculate the politics of cultural expression. Traditionally, they have used domesticity and its cultural offspring (denominated variously as "sentimentalism," "women's fiction," or "the domestic novel") in order to demarcate a stable divide between a "subversive" high cultural tradition and a "conservative" popular cultural tradition in the United States with origins in the mid-nineteenth century. Taking their cue from Melville's "Hawthorne and His Mosses," literary historians argued that "classic" writers used the conventions of women's best-sellers in order to communicate their own original and profound meanings. In this account, only the disempowered, male writers had the self-consciousness required to stand outside of social doxa; women writers dominated cultural production precisely because of their intellectual prostration before popular belief systems like domesticity.

The perdurability of this critical judgment, expressed most tren-chantly in Ann Douglas's *The Feminization of American Culture* (1977), is remarkable. Richard H. Brodhead, for example, wrote in 1986 in *The School of Hawthorne* that Herman Melville "worked in the same . . . literary and social milieu" as the domestic novelists, "but . . . stands not just in a different but in virtually the opposite relation to [domestic fiction] and its cultural accommodations."[1] The underexamined equa-tion of domesticity with unthinking conformity even led one prominent critic working under the auspices of Women's Studies to use woman-hood as the other against which she defined the classics. In an article first published in the feminist journal *Signs,* Myra Jehlen could claim, with-out anything resembling a sustained reading of domestic fiction, that nineteenth-century women writers could not compete artistically with Melville and the like because "no woman can assume herself because she has yet to create herself, and this the sentimentalists, acceding to their society's definition did not do." Jehlen wrote:

> To the extent that they began by taking the basic order of things as given, [the sentimentalists] forswore any claim on the primary vi-sion of art and saw themselves instead as interpreters of the estab-lished ethos, its guardians, or even, where needed, its restorers. . . . [Melville, on the other hand] could take on sentimentalism because he had an alternative world on which to stand: himself. [Hence, Melville's] *Pierre* does not know how to be acquiescently sentimen-tal, it can only be *about* sentimentalism.[2]

High culture's steadfast and univocal oppositionality in such analy-ses depends upon taking for granted the accommodative nature of all matters domestic, and hence all matters "feminine." Indeed, a long-standing critical legacy has made domesticity and the status quo virtually synonymous.

If the desire to locate the "classics" safely outside of power animates orthodox literary criticism, Anglo-American feminist criticism has, conversely, imagined home as a refuge from the forces of normalization. In her groundbreaking book *Sensational Designs* (1985), Jane Tompkins responded to the traditional demonization of domesticity (and the larger mass cultural tradition of which it forms a part) by asserting that "the popular domestic novel of the nineteenth century represents a monumental effort to reorganize culture from the woman's point of view" and that domestic fiction "in certain cases . . . offers a critique of American society far more devastating than any delivered by better-known critics such as Hawthorne and Melville." Tompkins's understanding of the politics of domesticity more generally makes possible her specific claims for the countercultural status of domestic fiction. As conceived by women intellectuals like Catharine Beecher and her sister and coauthor Harriet Beecher Stowe, the middle-class home is an *alternative* economic system, "one which," Tompkins proposed, "calls into question the whole structure of [a] society" whose values were increasingly determined by an escalating industrial-commercial economy.[3]

Most recently, critics inspired by the burgeoning field of ethnic and third world feminist criticism and theory have implicitly and explicitly challenged Tompkins's work by bringing attention to the class- and race-impelled subtexts—and the institutional contexts—of Anglo-American domesticity. In 1992 Laura Wexler voiced a position shared, presumably, by a number of what we might call revisionary feminists when she insisted that the "[Ann] Douglas-Tompkins debate . . . tended to elide, the expansive, imperial project of sentimentalism." Marshalling compelling evidence, Wexler urged:

> The energies [sentimentalism] developed were intended as a tool for the control of others. . . . This element of the enterprise was not oriented toward white, middle-class readers and their fictional alter egos at all, either deluded and hypocritical *or* conscious and seriously committed "to an ethic of social love." . . . Rather, it aimed at the subjection of different classes and even races.[4]

Complementing and inspiring Wexler's analysis, a recent series of studies describe how African American women writers (particularly those active in an abolitionist movement in which white, middle-class women had a significant presence) self-consciously appropriated the conventions of the discourse of domesticity in order to communicate their critique of the racism and sexism of the Northern, white middle classes. Hazel V. Carby's discussion of Harriet Jacobs in *Reconstructing*

Womanhood is paradigmatic in this respect; there Carby argues that "in order to retain narrative authority and to preserve a public voice acceptable to an antebellum readership," *Incidents in the Life of a Slave Girl* (1861) "carefully negotiated the tension between satisfying moral expectations" and "challenging" conventions of a middle-class womanhood "bound to a racist, ideological system." Jacobs's compromises with middle-class womanhood were self-conscious, part of a strategy through which she "demystified a convention that appeared as the obvious, commonsense rules of behavior and revealed the concept of true womanhood to be an ideology."[5]

The figure of the domestic woman has haunted us for over two centuries because of her utility for overstabilizing the analytic terms "ideology" and "opposition." No matter which side of the binarism contemporary critics place her on, she still serves the same purpose she serves in domesticity itself: defining (either through her presence or renunciation) a literary space insulated from politics. The nineteenth century called this place "home." We call it either "high culture" or "the margins." And if we characterize a high cultural or a marginal literary tradition as "political," we mean only that it resists or demystifies some ideological construct external to it.

Even though differences of persuasiveness and political investment distinguish the three critical stances outlined above, there is a consistency in the way in which diverse critical cohorts have imagined oppositionality and hegemony, and authorial transcendence serves in all three as the criterion for literary value. The aim of *Home Fronts* in relation to the critical legacy I have just sketched out, therefore, is neither to defend domesticity as a form of cultural expression nor to join the call for an expanded canon; rather, the book's goal is to inquire into the theoretical assumptions about power and resistance underlying contemporary debates about dominant and oppositional cultures.

These debates proceed from the assumption that culture either frees or enslaves. There appear to be no other choices. We seem unable to entertain the possibility that traditions, or even individual texts, could be radical on some issues (market capitalism, for example) and reactionary on others (gender or race, for instance). Or that some discourses could be oppositional without being outright liberating. Or conservative without being outright enslaving. If a tradition identified as "subversive" appears contaminated by the "dominant" culture, then we exculpate the author-hero(ine) by invoking Melvillian parody, textual depth, and self-consciousness. Melville, who fancied himself part of an Anglo-European "brotherhood" of writers extending back to Shakespeare, would be shocked to discover that, in contemporary criticism, "hoodwinking" the "superficial skimmer[s] of pages" had become the prerogative of African American women, but the drama of authorial high consciousness requires the irony.[6] Literary value seems to depend upon identification of idealized agents (authors or intellectuals) who stand outside the social and political ideologies of their time. The construction of this ideal agency also seems to demand the existence of another group (authors, readers) completely without agency vis-à-vis these same ideologies. Indeed, that group's utter subjection is just the inverse of the exaggerated agency given to the idealized author.

Mine may sound like an appeal to moderation or interpretive pluralism, but it is nothing so banal. Study of nineteenth-century culture seems to have consistently organized itself around binarisms (dominant / marginal, conservative / countercultural, unconscious / self-reflexive, active / passive). Such dyads ensue, I would claim, from what Michel Foucault characterizes as our tendency to understand both power and resistance as centralized, uniform, and static—easily abstracted from the specific social relations and institutional contexts through which they work. Repeatedly, critics have attempted to identify in one tradition or another (the "classics," women's domestic fiction, African American writing) a "single locus of great Refusal, [a] soul of revolt."[7] Unless one thinks of society as a monolithic whole against which must arise an equally monolithic opposition, then a progressive stance in one arena does not entail a progressive view in all other arenas. And the work performed by culture would not consistently affect the entire range of relationships of power, extending from the sexual to the international realm. If, following Foucault, we view hegemony not as a monolithic "structure" radiating from a single source but instead as a web of "non-egalitarian and mobile" power relations (Foucault 93), then we can better understand the seeming incommensurability of political visions represented in early-nineteenth-century texts—and perhaps temper our disappointment when we realize that authors have not done the impossible, that is, discovered the one key for the liberation of all humankind.

Foucault's *History of Sexuality: An Introduction* guides my interpretation of the culture of domesticity, but recent work on the intersections

of race, gender, and sexual identities also exerts its influence throughout *Home Fronts*. Creative writers and cultural theorists have brought
attention to the particular kind of disenfranchisement faced by women,
gays, and lesbians of color in the ethnic separatist movements in the
1960s and 1970s. Cherríe Moraga, for example, reports in her autobiography that the Chicano Movement ostensibly pitted those without
power (Mexican Americans) against those with it (Anglo-Americans).
But, as Moraga points out, if one factors in nontraditional political
categories like gender and sexuality, then both ally and enemy are not so
"easy to name." Then "power no longer breaks down into neat little
hierarchical categories, but becomes a series of starts and detours."[8] As
much as Foucault's work, the work of writers like Moraga leads one to
question the "binary and all-encompassing opposition between rulers
and ruled at the root of power relations" (Foucault 94).

This binarism has apparently determined critical perceptions of
early-nineteenth-century culture, even revisionist studies which take
nontraditional political categories like gender and race into account.
Because ideology is always embodied in particular semantics, issues,
contexts, and institutions, neither male nor female writers, neither
white, middle-class women nor African American women intellectuals
experienced it as a whole, abstract entity which they either rejected or
embraced. If one cannot stand entirely "outside" of ideology, then one
cannot stand entirely "inside" of it either. People operating with similar
assumptions, values, and vocabularies can be motivated by different
commitments and come to different conclusions, although that "difference" does not express the triumph of individualism, innovation, or
genius so much as the complexity of authors' social positionality and the
volatility of the rhetorical, historical, and material circumstances compelling the authorial enterprise.

All of the texts covered in this study are implicated, albeit differently,
in one of the most entrenched value systems of early-nineteenth-
century bourgeois society. But that fact does not deplete them of political or imaginative differences altogether; within the discursive param-
eters which *house* them all, they acquire their own, highly contingent
fronts for mediating cultural, social, and political conditions.

The following chapters use the example of early-nineteenth-century
domesticity to demonstrate that the politics of culture reside in local
formulations—and in the social and historical locations of those formu-

lations—rather than in some essential and ineluctable political tendency inhering within them. Instead of a monumental and centralized struggle between mind-numbing popular doctrine and demystifying marginal critique, *Home Fronts* describes different horizons of representation on which struggles for authority played themselves out in the antebellum period: the middle-class home, the frontier, African American activism, social reform movements, and homosocial high culture.

Chapter 1, an overview of the literary and historical materials, provides the reader with a sense of the scope of women's early-nineteenth-century writing on domesticity, both fictional and nonfictional. It lays out key contexts, concepts, and grammars—expanded and reworked in subsequent chapters—but also stresses difference, contradiction, and dissent within the culture of domesticity. The inextricability of domesticity from its expressions and receptions accounts for the elasticity of discursive materials which are nevertheless related to each other through dynamics of influence and dialogue. Acknowledging this plurality undermines the received equation of a "feminine" mass culture and blind allegiance to the status quo. Nineteenth-century representations of women's increasing authority (if not outright "control") over society have helped make this equation persuasive, but those representations are part of the discourse of domesticity itself. In failing to exercise sufficient skepticism towards the antebellum period's narrative of itself, I argue, contemporary cultural histories have reproduced its tropes of female power and masculine resistance, and these tropes motivate their search for an illusory position of powerlessness from which a purely oppositional literature could arise.

Chapter 2 addresses in a more sustained way the tendentious use of domestic womanhood in order to construct a "feminine" mass culture in the antebellum period. James Fenimore Cooper's critique of the domestic woman in *The Last of the Mohicans* (1826) depends, ironically, on domesticity's own narrative of modernization in which a centralized, patriarchal force is displaced by a dispersed, maternal authority—the latter symbolized in Cooper both by the middle-class home and by the rise of mass culture. Using as evidence the chain of connections that Cooper and his contemporaries forged between the domestic woman, expansionism, and modernity, I argue that despite their apparent antipodality, home and frontier worked together in building Jacksonian-era expansionism. Cooper, however, erases the memory of imperialism by identifying the domestic woman and the culture over which she presides as the source of oppression in the modern regime of social relations. The interpretation of the literary and historical materials then leads me to complicate New Historicist critiques of the politics of women's culture, and I conclude by suggesting that our own failure to historicize the trope of "feminine" disciplinary power provided by critics of domesticity like Cooper implicates us in his culture's expansionist logic.

My account in Chapter 2 of how a particular critique of the domestic woman ensures the erasure of people of color from the imaginative landscape by no means excludes Anglo-American domesticity from this process. In Chapter 3 the tense relation between Anglo-American domesticity and the political aspirations of people of color leads me to question why early black nationalist writer and lecturer Maria W. Stewart relied upon domesticity to justify her own career as a lecturer on racial injustice and women's rights in the early 1830s. The relative autonomy of Boston's black activist community from the later integrated abolitionist movement makes me suspect that Stewart was less interested in exposing domesticity as (to paraphrase Carby) a racist and class-bound ideological system than she was in using it to negotiate within the less asymmetrical power relations obtaining between African American men and African American women. Stewart found in Anglo-American domesticity's nationalist vision of social housekeeping a means of claiming citizenship in an African American political community that, like so many subaltern nationalisms, used manhood as its trope of citizenship. Reading Stewart's almost forgotten speeches is, I believe, crucial to understanding why assumptions about political resistance often compel scholars writing about African American culture to disown women's labor in nationalist movements. Stewart's manifest insightfulness into both race and gender hierarchies, however, does not fundamentally dismantle Anglo-American domesticity's gendered tropes of resistance and oppression. In fact, those tropes allow her to speak—and to speak in a contestatory voice—even if they at the same time mark the limitations of womanist politics.

Chapter 4 returns to the topic of womanist politics through readings of Anglo-American domesticity in Catharine Beecher's *Treatise on Domestic Economy* (1841) and Harriet Beecher Stowe's *Uncle Tom's Cabin* (1852). The chapter develops and complicates the identification of domesticity as a protofeminist critique of the patriarchal family by placing both Beecher's work and Stowe's novel within the rise of a regime of power facilitated through the middle-class medicine and education: bio-politics. Writing Beecher and Stowe into this history, however, does not prove that bio-politics makes "slaves" of us all; working with very similar assumptions about the government of the self, the two sisters articulate very different stands on the issue of abolition. I use that difference as a platform for working through claims, on the one hand, for the subversiveness of domesticity and, on the other, for its disciplinary nature. I conclude that what critical theory needs is a theory of oppositionality that does not define resistance as radical alterity modeled on an idealized liberal self, but instead one that can acknowledge both the value and limitations of political interventions performed by texts constitutionally compromised by decentralized social authority.

Chapter 5 engages the critique of domesticity in relation to that modernist literary icon: the self-reflexive text. Midcentury male abjection in a culture industry allegedly controlled by women has been the foundation for the construction of high culture. Critics have identified male alienation from the home as the origin of a protomodernist literary style that disrupts all received cultural values by estranging readers from the familiar; however, pressure on Nathaniel Hawthorne's trope of defamiliarization in the fluctuating and mutually constitutive registers of gothic and domestic in *The Scarlet Letter* (1850) yields evidence of the dependence of Hawthorne's self-reflexive text on the protocols of the nineteenth-century sex/gender system. It is, I assert, upon power relations entirely grounded in the history of the male homosocial culture of letters of Hawthorne's time that critics build claims for a literary style which dismantles power.

Whether celebrated or abjected, the discourse on the domestic structures antebellum representations of a variety of sites conflict. Antebellum authors use gender difference to stabilize categorical distinctions generated by their texts, including the opposition between power and resistance. As I will explain in the Conclusion, traditional constructions of the canon substitute restatement of this binary and gendered opposition for a genuinely analytic interpretation of cultural politics—one which could acknowledge the multiplicity of inequalities in society and the mobility of political meanings produced by the same discourse deployed within different kinds of power relations. Even as it strives to promote reading of neglected authors, nontraditional criticism augments the binary opposition between dominant and marginal, upon which rest modernist visions of the literary as the antithesis of the political.

Criticism continues to profit from assessments of canon-formation from feminist and minority standpoints. *Home Fronts,* however, instigates a distinct project: conceptualizing the value of noncanonical texts within a micropolitical framework. Other periods and other cultural materials demand interpretation within the critical-theoretical project undertaken in this book; however, as a form of cultural expression characteristic of middle-class women, early-nineteenth-century domesticity particularly necessitates a method of analysis responsive to privileges that do not amount to dominance and disenfranchisements that do not constitute powerlessness.[9]

1 & A SOCIETY CONTROLLED
BY WOMEN: AN OVERVIEW

It was not strange . . . that the household gods should be worshiped in a society controlled by women. . . . To this feminine world with home as its all-engrossing center, the domestic novelists made their chief appeal. Mobilized to defend and extol household virtues, battalions of women novelists advanced, and gained such numbers and influence that by the middle of the century they completely dominated the field. —H. Ross Brown, The Sentimental Novel in America[1]

Feminist rereadings of literary historical periods often proceed from the assumption that women writers were excluded from the production of the canon. In the construction of the antebellum canon, however, "deployment" rather than "exclusion" better describes the fate of women's fiction. Traditional literary histories of the period do not ignore women writers so much as use them as the other which endows the "classics" with their identity.[2]

Challenging the oppositional logic through which women have been simultaneously written out of and written into this cultural history requires a complex set of critical strategies. As H. Ross Brown's vision of female masses in military formation indicates, the opposition is richly sedimented, not just with the proprieties of gender and assumptions about mass culture but also with convictions about hegemony and resistance. This chapter dislodges some of the accumulated sediment of cultural history—first, by disputing the factual basis for claims of women's predominance in the cultural realm; second, by demonstrating critics' failure to recognize their perpetuation of the antebellum period's own dubious narrative about itself; and finally, by surveying women's cultural production in order to show how contentious and internally contested the apparently conventional and monolithic popular doctrine of domesticity really was.

The "Flood" Revisited

Significantly, twentieth-century literary historians' use of a rhetoric of gender in the construction of the American Renaissance derives from the work of canonical male writers of the period. For example, in *The Spy,* James Fenimore Cooper (who published his first novel under a female pseudonym) satirizes the literary predilections of "our country-women, by whose opinions it is that we expect to stand or fall."[3] Hawthorne's complaint that "America is now wholly given over to a d——d mob of scribbling women" has a talismanic status in the twentieth-century criticism, standing, as it does, at the foundation for so many interpretations of the period.[4] Taking these and other obviously tendentious statements at face value, H. Ross Brown made the patently absurd statement that the mid-nineteenth-century United States was "a society controlled by women."

Even literary historians less prone to hyperbole than Brown typically predicate both the singularity and subversiveness attributed to male authors not upon the development of mass culture but more specifically upon a mass culture dominated by women. The concept of the mid-nineteenth-century "classic" demands the existence of what Ann Douglas called "the feminization of American culture," that is, "the well-nigh dictatorial power middle-class women exerted over their culture."[5] Critics and literary historians usually begin by assuming "the standard view": "that between 1800 and 1860 America was flooded with novels and poetry volumes, written mainly by women and for women." But, according to David S. Reynolds, there has been a "widespread miscomprehension of antebellum women's culture and popular literature." Reynolds maintains that, in point of fact, women's culture enjoyed nothing like the dominance routinely attributed to it.[6]

Indeed, no direct proof corroborates Cooper's assertion that the success or failure of a novel depended on women's tastes. The characterization of the audience for novels as primarily female rests primarily upon indirect validation like that found in the introduction to *The Spy.* Cathy N. Davidson's *Revolution and the Word: The Rise of the Novel in America* contains the most scholarly and convincing work done on the gender composition of readership in the early United States. She writes that "all the material evidence available—extant lending-library rosters, subscription lists published in novels, and inscriptions found in extant copies of novels—attests that men as well as women read even the most sentimental novels," but unfortunately her study concludes with the 1820s.[7] No scholar has attempted to verify his or her claims about the gender composition of the antebellum novel-reading audience through primary data on a scale comparable to Davidson's. Douglas substitutes anecdote for evidence, relying on statements by "numerous [contemporaneous] observers" who reported that "countless young Victorian women spent much of their middle-class girlhoods prostrate on chaise longues with their heads buried in 'worthless' novels" (9).[8] So vital to the construction of the "classic" is the idea encapsulated in the phrase "the feminization of American culture" that the eminent William Charvat, while confessing that "no one knows what percentage of the readers of poetry, fiction, and essays was female," nevertheless insisted that "by 1851 women had become the chief consumers of fiction in America."[9]

Assertions that women dominated literary production appear as dubious as the claims made about their role in cultural consumption. Reynolds finds evidence that at midcentury men authored more than twice as much fiction as women.[10] Midcentury women writers like Warner, Stowe, and Maria Cummins (who wrote the first best-sellers in the modern sense of the term) far outsold the "classic" male novelists with whom they are usually compared; however, Hawthorne, Melville, and Cooper were not the only male novelists of the period. William Ware, T. S. Arthur, and Donald Mitchell are just a few of the male novelists whose popularity rivaled that of their female competitors. Lucy M. Freibert and Barbara A. White observe that "if women authored the top three sellers of the [nineteenth] century, men outnumbered women on the list three to one."[11] Finally, even if (as it indeed appears) the best-selling novels of the period written by women outsold the best-sellers written by men, the book-publishing industry was almost entirely in the hands of men, a fact that greatly complicates the issue of who "controlled" the literary marketplace.[12]

No doubt, conviction that the antebellum reading audience was increasingly (if not overwhelmingly) female in part explains traditional scholarly consensus that the general population of readers dismissed any novel threatening the literary, moral, or political conventions permitting them to proceed through their lives with as little reflection as possible.[13] But feminist criticism is just as likely to take for granted the standard view of literary history. At this moment criticism on ante-bellum culture seems to have distilled itself into a debate about whether the reign of white middle-class women through their domestic power base either fostered or prevented progressive cultural politics; however, the unreliable evidence on which female sovereignty in the cultural arena rests suggests the need for an entirely different line of inquiry, one exploring the nineteenth-century basis of twentieth-century critical belief. For, as I argue below, the reign of woman is a cultural artifact produced by the antebellum period: a domestic fiction whose plot unfolds across a range of fictional and nonfictional sources, a narrative which critics have unwittingly reified.

Female Influence and Male Counterculture

How is it that nineteenth-century cultural authorities like Hawthorne came to believe that "America ha[d] been wholly given over" to women?

The conviction seems to grow out of exaggerated claims for the influence—indeed, the all-powerfulness—of women generated by the rise of domesticity. By 1830 the nature of woman's contribution to society had become a regional obsession among Anglo-American intellectuals of the Northeastern United States, and by virtue of the dominance of this region's population over cultural production, it necessarily became a national obsession as well.

The Revolutionary-era idea of republican motherhood is in some sense the precursor of domesticity. The Enlightenment tenet that youth was particularly susceptible to both good and bad influences led late-eighteenth-century educators in the United States like Judith Sargent Murray and Benjamin Rush to argue that in their capacity as mothers women exercised a determining power over the fate of the Republic in the values they taught boys who would grow up to lead the nation. It was therefore necessary, argued these writers, to pay more attention to women's education than had previously been given, lest mothers communicate undemocratic dispositions to their male offspring.[14]

Whereas Murray and Rush attempted to incorporate women into the ongoing Revolutionary project by representing men and women as *equally* (but differently) capable of contributing to the moral well-being of the Republic, early-nineteenth-century writers increasingly enunciated womanhood as the *sole* repository of national virtue. At the same time that they began characterizing men as naturally aggressive, sensual, and godless, authors of countless speeches and publications began to argue that if women did not exercise a civilizing influence on male household members, society would collapse into complete anarchy. In one of the scores of sermons bearing the title "Female Influence" written in the period, the Reverend J. F. Stearns proclaimed to his women parishioners in 1837, "Yours it is to decide . . . whether we shall be a nation of refined and high minded Christians, or whether . . . we shall become a fierce race of semi-barbarians."[15]

While such theories of female influence held that women ultimately controlled society, they also stressed that women exercised that power through indirect influence rather than direct force. Before she married Nathaniel Hawthorne, Sophia Peabody (who found it "shock[ing] to have women mount the rostrum") expressed her belief that home was "the great arena for women [to] wield a power which no king or conqueror can cope with."[16] "The strength of man's character," wrote magazinist and novelist Sarah Hale in 1837, "is in his physical propensities—the strength of woman lies in her moral sentiments." If women sought to influence society directly (through, for example, agitating for the right to vote), they would lose their control over men, since brute force rather than moral suasion governed the political realm. Women's physical delicacy, Hale believed, would prevent them from competing with men on their own terms. Thus from her point of view it was in a woman's own best interest to remain within her "proper sphere":

> Authority over the men must . . . never be usurped; but still, women may, if they will, exert their talents and [by] opportunities nature has furnished, obtain an influence in society that will be paramount to authority. They may enjoy the luxuries of wealth, without enduring the labors to acquire it; and the honors of office, without feeling its cares, and the glory of victory, without suffering the dangers of the battle.[17]

For some writers, even moral suasion within her proper sphere was too direct a manifestation of woman's power. Child's 1831 treatise *The*

Mother's Book asserts that it is better for mothers to instruct through the example of their own virtuous behavior rather than through precept. Child (herself a novelist) recommended the reading of uplifting fiction, but she took care to distinguish uplifting fiction from fiction with a "good moral": "The morality should be *in* the book," she wrote, "not tacked upon the *end* of it."[18]

Its dialogic form made the novel a particularly appropriate vehicle for what the age defined as women's proper exercise of power. No doubt Maria Cummins was thinking of the educational uses to which her own work might be put when, in her novel *The Lamplighter* (1854), she describes Emily Graham judiciously selecting uplifting narratives of the "triumph of truth, obedience and patience" for Gerty Flint to read. This method of inculcating moral principles in her willful ward conforms with Emily's more general commitment to exerting her authority only covertly—a method contrasted with her father's disastrously manifest exertions of his authority. Emily, writes Cummins, "preached no sermons, nor did she weary [Gerty] with exhortations and precepts. Indeed, it did not occur to Gerty that she [was being] *taught* anything; but simply and gradually [Emily] imparted light to the child's dark soul."[19]

Because narrative was not considered rhetorical (rhetoric being associated with the "masculine" political sphere), writing fiction was seen as a particularly appropriate way for women to exert their indirect influence for the good of society.[20] Domesticity and its appropriation of narrative provide a context in which to understand Hawthorne's comment that his country had been taken over by a mob of women (a comment prompted specifically by the success of *The Lamplighter*). Hawthorne's overstatement of the case was informed as much by his culture's belief in the feminization of modern society as it was by his own professional jealousy. In fact, in *The Scarlet Letter*, five years before writing the letter to his publisher, Hawthorne suggested that the masculine-identified characteristics of Puritan times (the physical vigor and moral callousness of the Puritan elders) had given way to feminine-identified qualities of antebellum times (the exquisite delicacy and sensitivity of the narrator of "The Custom-House"). *The Scarlet Letter* describes even the Puritans as more "feminine" than their ancestors. Of the Puritan women who gather in the marketplace to witness Hester's public humiliation, the narrator believes that

[m]orally, as well as materially, there was a coarser fibre in those wives and maidens of old English birth and breeding, than in their fair descendants, separated from them by a series of six or seven generations; for, throughout that chain of ancestry, every successive mother has transmitted to her child a fainter bloom, a more delicate and briefer beauty, and a slighter physical frame, if not a character of less force and solidity, than her own. The women, who were now standing about the prison-door, stood within less than half a century of the period when the man-like Elizabeth had been the not altogether unsuitable representative of the sex.[21]

The theory that society had grown more feminine was by no means limited to male novelists of the period. Cooper, Hawthorne, and Melville manifested more hostility toward the changes they perceived than did most of the women writers represented in this study. And one could argue, as many critics have, that the classic male writers evidenced their hostility in plots revolving around the flight of male characters into the wilderness or out to sea (and thus away from the rule of women). A reading of women's texts, however, complicates the association of this theme of gendered flight with writerly rebellion against modern "feminization."

Take the example of Stowe's *The Pearl of Orr's Island* (1862), a historical romance set, like *The Scarlet Letter,* in Puritan times. Stowe perhaps alludes to *The Scarlet Letter* by referring to her young female protagonist as the "pearl," the name Hawthorne gave to Hester Prynne's daughter. In Stowe's novel, the adolescent male protagonist, Moses Pennel, begins to chafe at his virtuous female friend Mara Lincoln's apron strings. Moses, explains the narrator,

> could n't be expected to think as much of her as she of him. He was handsomer, cleverer, and had a thousand other things to do and to think of—he was a boy, in short, and going to be a glorious man and sail all over the world, while she could only hem handkerchiefs and knit stockings, and sit at home and wait for him to come back.

But Stowe's narrator, prophesying the situation that nineteenth-century Americans felt increasingly characteristic of their own century, associates seventeenth-century New England with the haughty masculinity of the young Moses and coyly confides to her readers: "There may, perhaps, come a time when the saucy boy, who steps so superbly, and predominates so proudly in virtue of his physical strength and daring, will learn to tremble at the golden measuring-rod, held in the hand of a woman."[22]

This reading of *The Pearl of Orr's Island* suggests that women's novels already contain the narrative of male rebellion against the rule of women that is generally attributed to male writers. Moses Pennel's decision to go to sea to sow his wild oats anticipates Huck Finn's resolution at the end of *The Adventures of Huckleberry Finn* to "light out" for the Western frontier in order to evade his aunt's "sivilizing" designs on him. In other words, far from undermining domesticity, male narrations of rebellion against women's rule reiterate domesticity's association of men with "semi-barbarism" and women with "high minded" Christianity.

Similarly, I would argue that twentieth-century accounts of the antebellum period in which the classic male novelists personify rebellion against acceptable conventions are simply rewritings of domestic ideology in which "masculine" lawlessness is redefined as individualism, vigor, and political subversion, and "feminine" goodness is redefined as dependence, enervation, and capitulation. In *Manhood in the American Renaissance,* for example, David Leverenz refers to "American literature's Great Divide, the split between popular women's literature and canonized men's texts," and he juxtaposes readings of Emerson, Thoreau, Melville, and Hawthorne with readings of Susan Warner, Harriet Beecher Stowe, Sarah Hale, and Caroline Kirkland. Yet, far from interrogating the divide to which it refers, *Manhood in the American Renaissance* reasserts it by stating that male writers' "self-consciousness of being deviant from prevailing norms of manhood" led to their collective "alienated imagination" and resulted in the string of male classics known as the "American Renaissance." Such "nonconformity was," according to Leverenz, "unavailable to women writers"—except for a handful who "were [not] afraid to challenge social expectations." Conspicuous among Leverenz's account of the sources of female timidity is fear "of the stigma brought on by deviance from women's proper domestic role": "middle-class women . . . wanted above all else to be, as the reigning phrase put it, polite, refined, and Christian."[23] Since Leverenz also claims that only a handful of male artists challenged social expectations (and thereby produced the American Renaissance), his articulation of opposition along the lines of gender seems gratuitous—except inasmuch as it represents a familiar critical attempt to guarantee the countercultural status of "classic" male writers. The critical enterprise of defining a classic tradition against women writers reifies rather than analyzes the antebellum era's own habit of conceptualizing authority and rebellion through the representational matrix of middle-class gender norms.

Domesticity as Ideology and Resistance

Reiterations of the gendered figures of power and resistance appearing in both classic and popular antebellum texts hamper prefeminist studies of the period. But first-wave feminist attempts, like critic Jane Tompkins's, to reverse the values of literary history by asserting that women's writing represents the genuinely subversive tradition do not fundamentally disrupt the logic of domesticity either; they just restore domestic women to the station of moral and political transcendence they allotted to themselves.

By introducing categories such as class and race into the discussion, revisionary feminist criticism has usefully problematized this cultural / critical tendency to use gender binarisms in order to stabilize the distinction between power and resistance. Revisionary feminist accounts bring attention to gender, class, and race as competing and intersecting determinates of ideological subscription / transcendence. Still, there does seem to be a structuring assumption uniting revisionary feminist work with the earlier approaches in that, for all three, the author's relationship to ideology (domestic or otherwise) is always a zero-sum game; any involvement means total capitulation and any critique signals complete demystification.

Ideologies like domesticity become popular, I would argue, not because they provide the masses with a finite and orderly set of beliefs relieving them from the burden of thinking but instead because they give people an expansive logic, a meaningful vocabulary, and rich symbols through which to *think* about their world.[24] Like literary critic Mary Poovey, I will stress the "uneven" nature of ideology, its being "both contested and always under construction; because it [is] always in the making, it [is] always open to revision, dispute, and the emergence of oppositional formulations."[25]

The cult of domesticity may have become culturally dominant by the

mid-nineteenth century, but it is important to bear in mind that, orig-
inally, it was an oppositional formulation. Domesticity's origins are
explicitly antipatriarchal, and while to argue this is not the same thing as
arguing that domesticity was feminist, radical, or even the best that
women could do under the circumstances, it does explain why so many
women took up the pen in behalf of a philosophy that seems, from a
contemporary perspective, so at odds with women's political, economic, and personal independence. Such women were neither victims
of false consciousness nor clever manipulators of an ideology forced
upon them and for which they had secret contempt.[26] Instead, they were
women who found in the antipatriarchal analysis of the family at the
heart of domesticity a compelling language for describing women's
second-class status and for imagining ways (some more efficacious than
others) of improving it. We need not call domesticity "feminist" in
order to appreciate its antipatriarchal motivations. Contemporary feminism is not reducible to a critique of the patriarchal family; by calling
domesticity feminist we prepare ourselves for disappointment over its
lack of radicalism at the same time that we obscure the interventionary
value that it did have.

Domesticity proceeds from a repudiation of the exchange of women
within the aristocratic patriarchal system. Jean-Jacques Rousseau cap-
tures the spirit of the patriarchal view of womanhood when he, in his
cursory treatment of female education in *Émile* (1762), explains the
difference between male education and female education as the difference between "the development of strength" and "the development of
attractiveness."[27] Responding in part to Rousseau in her *Strictures on the
Modern System of Female Education* (1799), British educator Hannah More
(who is generally credited with the founding of domestic ideology)
criticized her contemporaries for educating their daughters "for the
world, and not for themselves."[28] Patriarchal interests dictated the
shape of the system of female education More wanted to reform. Con-
sisting almost exclusively in ornamental graces requisite for obtaining an
advantageous familial alliance through the marriage contract, this education, More felt, treated women as little more than trophies exchanged
between male heads of households. Rousseau expressed the degree to
which women were raised "for the world" rather than for themselves
when he argued that a woman's knowledge and powers of reasoning
should be developed only enough so as to prevent her from being tedious

in conversation with her husband. Using the home as a metaphor for interiority (in the sense of "selfhood"), More was attempting to redefine woman's value in terms of internal qualities: sound judgment, knowledge of how to run a household, moral tendencies—qualifications that suited a woman to be a good wife and mother rather than merely making her satisfying to the male gaze.

Historical romances written by women clearly express domesticity's antipatriarchal content. We see this in Lydia Maria Child's romance of ancient Greece, *Philothea* (1836). Aspasia, who herself relentlessly cultivates the gaze of the crowd, holds entertainments at her home in which women dance and sing before a male audience. Child's retiring heroine Philothea, seemingly voicing the author's view, explains to Aspasia that the renown women gain from performing before men is a sign of their thralldom rather than a measure of their freedom. The presence in the narrative of a woman who is literally enslaved (Philothea's friend Eudora) only strengthens the force of an analogy that later antislavery novels like Stowe's *Uncle Tom's Cabin* (1852) and Child's *A Romance of the Republic* (1867), would pursue in a native and more contemporary setting.

Like *Philothea,* Eliza Buckminster Lee's *Parthenia* (1858) constructs the domestic woman in order to criticize patriarchy. Set in the fourth century, the novel describes the youth of Emperor Julian, who dedicated himself to reviving the worship of the pagan gods just as Christianity seemed on the verge of establishing its ascendancy. Lee transforms the struggle between paganism and Christianity into a struggle between men and women. The woman-hating warrior Julian believes that Christianity is a religion suited only to the "weaker" sex. In the biblical story of the crucifixion Julian sees only an affront to the code of male heroism he associates with Homeric literature. In meeting the beautiful and wise pagan priestess Parthenia, however, Julian learns firsthand that there are forms of power other than physical force. He proposes that she become his empress and use her feminine charms to promote the cause of paganism. Parthenia declines the honor. In her gradual conversion to Christianity she learns that the only way to make woman a "purifying and refining influence infused through society" is to "elevate [her] to her true place in the *family.*"[29] Through Julian's offer, Lee communicates the patriarchal drive to reduce women to mere objects for public display.

While one could read assertions of women's moral superiority as empowering to women, historical romances written by women suggest that because theirs is the power of influence rather than of force, domesticity is always on the verge of reproducing patriarchal culture's male gaze. More than a passion for realist detail motivates Stowe's observation in *Uncle Tom's Cabin* (1852) that the flush of anger on Mrs. Bird's "very red cheeks" while she criticizes her husband's support of the Fugitive Slave Act "quite improved her general appearance."[30] In *Oldtown Folks* (1869), Stowe suggests that women's power over men depends upon their ability to please. Her character Tina's spectacular beauty, far from being a source of temptation for Stowe's male characters, is instead presented as, potentially, an agent of their regeneration. The narrator speaks of romantic "LOVE" as the "greatest and holiest of all the natural sacraments and means of grace." Stowe contrasts this perspective with that of the Calvinist minister Dr. Stern, who believes that "the minister who does not excite the opposition of the natural heart fails to do his work."[31] Significantly, the minister's sermons excite only revulsion among the townsfolk. Stowe had previously relocated gospel authority from the clergy to the eroticized domestic woman in *The Minister's Wooing* (1859). In this other historical romance set in Puritan New England, James Marvyn asserts that he does not understand a word of the minister Dr. Hopkins's tedious sermons but that the lovely Mary Scudder is his "living gospel."[32]

Although thinking of women as the living gospel for men gives women a certain authority, it also defines them in terms of men's needs. Because domestic ideology posits a moral difference between men and women, it always threatens to reduce women to little more than vessels for male salvation. One could argue that Stowe's representation of the virtuous heroine not long for this world (the archetypal expression of which is, of course, Eva St. Clare in *Uncle Tom's Cabin*) results from the moral difference between the sexes required by domestic ideology. Referring to Mara Lincoln's little Eva-like demise at the end of *The Pearl of Orr's Island,* the narrator declares that some people die young in order to aid in the spiritual development of those whom they leave behind. Mara's death has this effect on her skeptical fiance Moses Pennel, whose salvation seems much more secure after her death than before it. In fact, on her deathbed Mara informs him, ". . . I may have more power over you, when I seem to be gone, than I should have had living."[33] For Stowe, then, a woman's dying gospel is perhaps even more potent than her living one.

Yet if domesticity helped produce these images of selfless women, it also criticized patriarchal culture for robbing women of their selfhood. More felt that what Rousseau conceived of as the properly feminine "art of getting looked at" prevented women from maintaining an identity autonomous from male sexual desire.[34] The life of the young lady, More lamented, "too much resembles that of an actress; the morning is all rehearsal, and the evening is all performance."[35] More's protégé in the United States, Catharine Beecher, used images of physical confinement to express patriarchal culture's violence against the integrity of female selfhood. Beecher authored what is probably the single most influential statement of domesticity, *A Treatise on Domestic Economy* (1841), which she later (with the aid of her sister Harriet Beecher Stowe) revised and published under the title *The American Woman's Home* (1869). In these and other works, Beecher expresses concern that young girls spend too much time indoors in overheated rooms and that when they are permitted outdoors are instructed not to "romp and run like boys." Corsets and other "monstrous fashions" further impede the natural growth and development of the body and "bring distortion and disease"—literally, to the female body but, metaphorically, to the female self.[36]

Louisa May Alcott was particularly sensitive to the performative nature of female identity in the patriarchal regime. "I hate," says tomboy Jo March in *Little Women* (1869), "to think I've got to grow up and be Miss March, and wear long gowns, and look as prim as a China-aster."[37] Similarly, *Behind a Mask: A Woman's Power* (1866) represents traditional womanhood as a product of costume and lighting, but in this novella Alcott turns what More and Beecher saw as the tragedy of womanhood into a comedy of female self-advancement. Set in an aristocratic English household, *Behind a Mask* features a Brontë-esque governess who skillfully manipulates her haughty, class-conscious employers so as to make herself indispensable to them. At the end of the first chapter, when Jean Muir relaxes alone after an impressive first day on the job, she proclaims aloud, "the curtain is down, so I may be myself for a few hours, if actresses ever are themselves." She then removes her makeup, wig, and several false teeth. The "metamorphosis was wonderful," remarks the narrator; the sprightly, gentle governess becomes a tired, bitter-countenanced hag.[38] Rendered by Jonathan Swift, the revelation of the monstrosity hidden beneath a facade of female beauty may be misogynist, but Alcott encourages identification with her unlikely heroine by exploiting the class and nationalist biases of her audience against the Coventrys. Ultimately, having seduced and married the male head of the household, Jean Muir gets what she has wanted all along: the whole, aristocratic Coventry family at *her* beck and call.

Interiority and Revaluation

In *The Bonds of Womanhood,* historian Nancy F. Cott interprets domesticity as an attempt to reinvest woman and home with some of the social status that they lost to declining household production and the related isolation of women and children. *Little Women* refigures the segregation of male and female spheres in reference to the Civil War. The March sisters remain at home, while the Northern men have gone "far away, where the fighting was." Jo rails against the destiny of her sex: "I'm dying to go and fight with papa, and I can only stay at home and knit like a poky old woman." Through her representation of the March sisters' struggle to "fight their bosom enemies bravely" and to "conquer themselves," Alcott endeavors to reinvest the home with value, relocating within its walls the heroism traditionally identified with the battlefield.[39] Alcott suggests that, in part because heroics attract the attention of the world, it is far easier to be a hero than it is to purify one's own heart; temporary hardship and even death in the name of a virtuous cause are more easily endured than a quiet, lifetime struggle for virtue.

During the Civil War years the influential women's magazine *Godey's Lady's Book* was an important vehicle for its editor Sarah Hale's very conservative domestic philosophy. Hale's detractors have taken the magazine's infrequent references to the major military conflict of the day as evidence that women intellectuals retreated to the home to escape harsh realities.[40] Indeed, Harriet Beecher Stowe described her *House and Home Papers,* a series of articles published in the *Atlantic Monthly* in 1864, as "a sort of spicy sprightly writing that I feel I need to write in these days to keep from thinking of things that make me dizzy & blind & fill my eyes with tears."[41] But Stowe's refusal to let Northerners avert their eyes from the crime of slavery in works like *Uncle Tom's Cabin, A Key to Uncle Tom's Cabin* (1853), and *Dred* (1856) in part made the reality of the Civil War. These women did not try to escape "reality"; they tried to redefine it to correspond with an antipatriarchal value system.

According to Child's *The Mother's Book,* "Nothing can be real that has not its home *within* us."[42] Addressing the question of discipline, *The Mother's Book* stresses that behavior matters far less than the motives that impel it. *Little Women* uses the backdrop of the Civil War to create a value system that gives priority not just to women but to women as the representatives of the interior life. The same reasoning that led Alcott to valorize the (feminine) quotidian over the (masculine) heroic led minister Horace Bushnell to propose a new "domestic" form of worship. Referring in part to the histrionic conversions accompanying the religious revivals that punctuated the entire antebellum period, in *Christian Nurture* (1847) Bushnell complained: "We hold a piety of conquest rather than of love,—a kind of public piety, that is strenuous and fiery on great occasions, but wants . . . constancy."[43] In Bushnell's opinion all Christians, not just women, should cultivate domesticity of character.

Thus the appearance of the domestic woman in the early nineteenth century cannot be separated from the modern reconstruction not just of the female self but of selfhood in general. Nancy Armstrong argues that, "the modern individual was first and foremost a female."[44] Armstrong exaggerates domesticity's hegemony; masculinist discourses constructed their own versions of subjectivity against female selfhood. And yet domesticity certainly articulated interiority as fundamentally feminine. Middle-class womanhood became the sign of a self underlying behavior and action.

The increasing conventionality of claims for women's domestic identity would seem to circumscribe their lives completely within that home, but, ironically, making domesticity into an identity gave middle-class women a surprising amount of mobility. As an identity rather than simply as a fixed location for women's lives, domesticity could—and did—travel. Women could argue that they continued to embody domesticity even when they left home. And domesticity's oppositional origins, its status as a discourse about oppression and resistance, determined that middle-class women's itineraries would include sites of social conflict and political struggle.

Contact Zones

Domesticity's valorization of motive over behavior gave novelists license to produce some of the era's most respectful representations of non–Anglo-European cultures. In *Hobomok* (1824) Child protests the undue harshness of Calvinist doctrine that would damn the unconverted but "noble" savage to everlasting punishment in the afterlife. *Hobomok* is a tale of interracial marriage. At one point Mary Corbitant, who marries Hobomok and bears his child, has a vision of the Christian God smiling "on distant mosques and temples" and "shedding the same light on the sacrifice heap of the Indian, and the rude dwellings of the Calvinist." The narrator lays the groundwork for an early theory of cultural relativism when she asserts that spiritual light shines equally on all people but is refracted in many different ways.[45] Child's representation of native culture leaves much to be desired, but at least in her case domesticity's values seem to have given her the opportunity to imagine an alternative to her contemporary James Fenimore Cooper's *The Last of the Mohicans* and other Jacksonian-era narratives about the perils of miscegenation and the "inevitable disappearance" of native peoples.

Of course, the willingness of women novelists to entertain notions of cultural relativism was not disinterested. Sedgwick's *Hope Leslie* (1827) employs relativism to buttress its own antipatriarchal critique as much as to ennoble aboriginals. Through the generous actions of her native heroine Magawisca, Sedgwick legitimates the alien culture rejected by the Puritan rulers because it does not conform to their ethnocentric standards. At the same time, and through a similar logic, Sedgwick legitimates acts of defiance against the Puritan elders committed by her white heroine Hope Leslie. Raised by a heterodox aunt, Hope doubts the "infallibility" of the Puritan authorities. "Like the bird that spreads his wings and soars above the limits by which each man fences in his own narrow domain, she enjoyed the capacities of her nature, and permitted her mind to expand beyond the contracted boundaries of sectarian faith." In an age of what Sedgwick calls "undisputed masculine supremacy," Hope fails to demonstrate the "passiveness" that the Puritans define as woman's chief virtue. Sedgwick describes Hope as someone whom the Puritans perceive as, like the natives, in need of "civilizing" restraints. But Hope's conduct only appears immoral; in fact, steadfast principles guide her actions throughout the novel: "Her religion was pure . . . no one, therefore, should doubt its intrinsic value, though it had not been coined into a particular form, or received the current impress."[46]

The domestic emphasis on character over conduct may also account for the frequency with which orphans appear in women's novels. In three of the most popular novels of the time, Warner's *The Wide, Wide World* (1850), Cummins's *The Lamplighter* (1854), and Martha Finley's *Elsie Dinsmore* (1867), the death of one or both parents or the abandonment of children is a compelling *donnée* for women novelists because it provides an opportunity for distinguishing between character and conduct. Only with the parent absent can the child's internalization of principle be gauged. As in Ralph Waldo Emerson's essay on the topic, self-reliance in women's novels refers to an internal standard of duty instead of freedom from duty. This is not to say that by internalizing duty domesticity merely introjected patriarchal rule, but rather to suggest that even critical discourses can normalize at the same time that they empower.

Interestingly, the first novel written by an African American in the United States is yet another story of an orphaned girl in search of "self-dependence." This child, however, is a mulatta living in the North, taken in as a servant when her impoverished white mother (ostracized because of her liaison with a black man) abandons her. Harriet E. Wilson's *Our Nig; or, Sketches from the Life of a Free Black* (1859), evokes all of the pathos of motherlessness that we see in Anglo-American novels. "I ha'n't got no mother, no home," declares her heroine Frado at the beginning of *Our Nig*. "I wish I was dead."[47]

Middle-class culture had made the bond between mother and child sacrosanct. Yet ostensibly middle-class values can communicate very different political meanings when enacted in specific narratives. In *Our Nig* both "self-dependence" and the longing for home specifically refer to the main character's experience with antebellum practices for managing indigent populations. As an orphaned child, Frado expresses her desires against the backdrop of indentured servitude. As an adult and a member of the working class, her desire for home and independence have meaning in the context of her experience of community assistance, which places her in various households, separates her from the child she cannot support, and renders both mother and child potentially subject to strangers' abuse and neglect in the future.

Critic Claudia Tate suggests that, because of the particularity with which race oppression expressed itself, the integrity of the domestic sphere became a particularly meaningful symbol of civil equality for African Americans. In the antebellum era, Tate notes,

slaves could not enter in legal marriage because they had no civil
status. . . . . The history of slavery as well as its literary representations record slaves marrying and practicing monogamy to the best
of their ability. However, such marriages were routinely dissolved
at the auction block where families were torn apart with bills of
sale.[48]

Abolitionist-sponsored slave narratives like Harriet Jacobs's *Incidents in
the Life of a Slave Girl* (1861) exposed Anglo-American readers to this
particular, politicized iconography of the decimated slave family; Wilson established its relevance for blacks in the North as well as in the
South.

Since Wilson (unlike Jacobs) apparently addressed her novel to other
free blacks,[49] she did not need sentimental conventions to appease a
skeptical, white audience. Reading works by free black women rather
than slave narratives makes African American women writers' relationship to domesticity look like something more complex than convenient
rhetorical manipulation. Maria W. Stewart, a free-born African American woman who lectured before black audiences in the early 1830s,
depended upon the concept of female influence to put black women at
the forefront of abolitionist and antiracist causes. Stewart observes "that
by prudence and economy in their domestic concerns, and their un-
wearied attention in forming the minds and manners of their children,"
white women had gained respect and influence in society. "Shall we not
imitate their examples . . . ?" she asked. Stewart encourages other
African American women to join her fight against racial and gender
prejudice and to wield female influence to further the good of the
nation. Stewart's debt to domesticity did not prevent her from making
it responsive to her particular political situation. Far from limiting
woman's influence to friends, family, and fiction, Stewart urges African
American women to "[plead] in public for our rights."[50]

Escalating sectional and racial conflict motivated other radical reinterpretations of domesticity as a justification for women's foray out of
their "proper sphere." Beginning in the 1850s, former slave turned
itinerant preacher and abolitionist lecturer, Sojourner Truth took up a
version of maternalist politics reminiscent of Stewart's.[51] "Robbed" by
slavery of her "own offspring," Truth is said to have "*adopted* her race"
in their stead. According to the *Narrative of Sojourner Truth* (as told to

Olive Gilbert and Frances W. Titus), Truth "regretted . . . that women had no political rights under government; for she knew that could the voice of maternity be heard . . . , the welfare, not only of the present generation, but of future ones, would be assured."[52]

The idea of political motherhood had a lasting impact on African American women's writing and activism. Tate describes an "alignment" of the identities of "wife, mother, and social reformer" in late-nineteenth-century African American women's fiction and nonfiction, one that "appropriates the entire world of Afro-American public and private affairs [into the] domain" of black women.[53] In 1892, Anna Julia Cooper wrote in *A Voice From the South* that "a race is but a total of families, the nation is the aggregate of its homes. . . . Only the BLACK WOMAN can say, 'When and where I enter, in the . . . undisputed dignity of my womanhood . . . then and there the whole *negro race enters with me.*'"[54] Joyce Hope Scott has even gone so far as to propose that, without recourse to the legitimating rhetoric of nineteenth-century domesticity, black women in the Civil Rights era lost their "earlier vocality and centrality" as a "phallocentric and patriarchal vision of Black Power [relocated] the black woman in the margins of the struggle for freedom and equality."[55]

Not all nineteenth-century African American women writers, however, shared the faith in the domestic woman's ability to bridge the gap between the public and the private. As a leader in efforts to aid freed slaves in the North during and after the Civil War, ex-slave Elizabeth Keckley had a personal stake in assessing the kind of indirect influence a woman could exercise in the public realm. Although her memoir tells us very little about her own experiences as an activist, Keckley seems to use the fate of her employer and confidante Mary Todd Lincoln to express her own sense of the limitations that domesticity placed on women's access to public affairs. Keckley relates in her memoir (published in 1869) that during her husband's term in office Mary Lincoln considered herself "Mrs. President" and freely offered her advice about matters of political strategy to him.[56] But in Keckley's account female "influence" is not particularly effective; Lincoln summarily dismisses his wife's advice. Moreover, after his assassination, the nation's reverence towards his memory did not extend to his widow, who found herself ridiculed in the press for failing to adhere to the norms of private womanhood.

From the Domestic to the Social

The growing sense of national crisis culminating in the Civil War also spurred Anglo-American reinterpretations of women's civilizing mission. Novelist Elizabeth Oakes Smith, for example, authored a series of articles for the New York *Tribune* in the 1850s in which she exhorted women to intervene in public and political matters. Smith conceded—indeed, insisted upon—the doctrine of separate spheres. Man's superior physical strength and his greater powers of reasoning and perseverance, she wrote, indicate that "God has appointed" man "*Lord of the material Universe.*" And woman's intuitiveness, beauty, and physical delicacy put her one "step nearer [to the angels] than her *material* lord and master." Working from the same assumptions about gender difference as more conservative women writers, Smith (like them) believed that women could "produce the new heavens and the new earth of the moral world." But, unlike her more conservative counterparts, Smith asserted that "the indefinite influence sprung from the private circle is not enough"; "the world goes on with its manifold wrongs, and woman has nothing but tears to bestow." How much better the world would be, reasons Smith, if woman could "enlarge her sphere" to include public as well as private affairs. "In the progress of events," she concludes, "I see no reason why the influence of woman should not be acknowledged at the ballot-box: indeed, when we consider the disorder and venality prevailing there, it would seem that her voice may be the great element needful to reform."[57] The ballot box became in some women's minds a means for realizing domesticity's reformist agenda. Whether or not domesticity was created "to placate women for their exclusion from the public sphere,"[58] it also "contained within itself the preconditions for organized feminism, by allotting a 'separate' sphere for women," giving them a gender-identified sense of social purpose, and providing access to associations in which they learned the procedures and skills for mobilizing public campaigns.[59]

Postwar suffragists like Elizabeth Cady Stanton followed Smith's eloquent example and used the logic of domesticity in their fight for women's political empowerment; however, the influence of domesticity on the suffragists guaranteed that early feminism would inherit its political liabilities. Differences of access to the means of cultural production meant that domesticity enunciated primarily the interests of white, middle-class women (a disenfranchised group, certainly, but by no means the only one). As early as 1838 in her *Letters to Mothers,* Lydia Sigourney attempted to expand the terrain of domesticity into the world at large. Appalled that "the influx of untutored foreigners" had made the United States "a repository for the waste and refuse of other nations," Sigourney maintained that it was the responsibility of women "to neutralize this mass" through an internal missionary movement that would spread the good word of the Anglo-American middle-class home.[60]

Postwar suffragists, retaining domesticity's vision of the custodial role of women, used an argument reminiscent of Sigourney's to press for the vote. If white middle-class women were enfranchised, they reasoned, it would offset the supposed deleterious influence of lower-class immigrants and recently emancipated slaves.[61] Even at the end of the nineteenth century, when domesticity seemed at last to have acquired a recognizably feminist character in its suffragist agenda, it was not in any simple sense liberating. The same millennial zeal which Cott claims gives domesticity its radical potential, also gives it a custodial mission with both classist and ethnocentric tendencies. Domesticity would continue to be "experienced differently by individuals who were positioned differently within the social formation (by sex, class, or race, for example)" and would continue to be "articulated differently by . . . different institutions, discourses, and practices."[62]

Declarations of women's moral superiority and civilizing influence, as well as claims for the managerial and practical skills they acquired through labor in the home, also paved the way for women's entry into professional careers. However "feminized" the careers to which women laid claim through domesticity would become, however underpaid and undervalued teaching, nursing, and social work were relative to "male professions," still these fields offered the economic independence without which modern feminism would be unimaginable.

In this regard Alcott's novel *Work* (1873) seems to mark both change and the continuity in the postwar period. The novel opens with the orphan Christie Devon announcing to her guardians that "there's going to be a new Declaration of Independence," namely, her declaration of economic independence from them. "I'm old enough to take care of myself; and if I'd been a boy, I should have been told to do it long ago," says Christie. "I hate to be dependent; and now there's no need of it, I can't bear it any longer."[63] Significantly, the kind of work that Alcott invents for her heroine is an extension of the domestic woman's responsibilities for peacekeeping and benevolence. Christie ultimately becomes a mediator in an organization composed of both middle- and working-class women. There she helps to heal the class conflicts that divide women. Alcott's fictional character Christie anticipates historical figures like Jane Addams, who at the turn of the century established social work as a legitimate profession for women. Because domesticity placed the welfare of society in women's able hands, they could claim social professions outside of the home as the logical extension of their work inside the home.

Alcott perceived that the particular skills, knowledge, and sensibilities women cultivated in managing households had extradomestic applications, and this perception no doubt influenced her own decision to become a nurse during the Civil War. Women doctors did not succeed as well as nurses did in making theirs into a "female profession." They did try, however. Dr. Mary Studley represented women's access to medical knowledge as a rebellion against patriarchal authority. Once women gain an understanding of "what is causing so much misery among them," wrote Studley in 1878,

> they find it difficult to wait in the [doctor's] office for the mischief to be done which they know is so much more easily prevented than cured; hence they go forth to the school and the lecture-room as missionaries and ministers of the goddess Hygeia, the fair daughter who put more faith in correct living than in the charmed serpents of her father Aesculapius.[64]

Domesticity's valorization of the quotidian enabled Studley to advocate preventive medicine (hygiene) over curative techniques (called the "heroic" system).

Dr. Elizabeth Blackwell attempted to enhance her own professional viability through a similar appeal to the quotidian. Although she wrote, seemingly with self-deprecation, that women physicians were best suited for "the study of the ordinary diseases of domestic life," she also believed that the heroic system of medicine had become virtually obsolete. Blackwell implied that women doctors, by virtue of their domesticity, had a particular aptitude in a modern medical profession which would increasingly stress healthy "habits . . . formed by . . . the silent working of influences, hour by hour and day by day, that are invisible and cannot be measured, that seem valueless, taking item by item . . . and yet in the aggregate . . . mould body and soul."[65] Professionalization of women's quotidian faculties, of course, meant access to institutions of higher learning. Blackwell, in fact, received the first medical degree granted to a woman in the United States.

Obviously, domestic ideology did not disappear with consolidation of the suffrage movement, with the expansion of professions for women, or with large-scale access for women to colleges and universities. The institutional context for domesticity, however, did undergo radical changes after the Civil War. Women's postwar agitation for the vote and their activities during the Civil War in semipublic organizations like the U.S. Sanitary Commission helped "[propel] autonomous, mass-based women's organizations into the nation's political mainstream." Domesticity's maternalist aspirations were gradually institutionalized, losing their grassroots foundation and increasingly becoming, in the 1890s, the skeletal structure upon which the nation built a system of social welfare.[66] Welfare bureaucracies absorbed women's custodial energies, and women in the "caretaking professions" developed a "new relationship to the state."[67]

The "social" is the term Jacques Donzelot uses to describe new knowledges and practices issuing from centralized governmental preoccupation with creating national standards of living.[68] Placed in the history presented in this chapter, however, the birth of the social represents a rebirth of domesticity, reconstructed by its authors as a rationale for women's participation in large-scale community and even national projects insuring the health and welfare of the population. The rationale had become conventional enough to make the dichotomy of home and world insufficient. As an intermediate term, "social" codified and legitimated women's activities outside of the home; at the same time it preserved them from a putatively "masculine" sphere of politics and power—even as women's custodial activities garnered widespread institutional and state support. On the other hand, critiques of intervention into the lives of citizens, conducted under the rubric of social welfare, would continue to represent power as a domestic plot, a product of the "feminization" of governmental functions.

The twentieth century would conduct its debates about women's authority through the language and practices of "the social" rather than those of "the domestic"; however, recourse to gender as a means of figuring both power and powerlessness clearly outlasted domesticity's antebellum heyday. Contemporary cultural criticism is another place where nineteenth-century narratives about gender, power, and resistance continue to be told. The chapters which follow give more thorough attention both to how the antebellum period deployed these narratives and to the question of why the figure of the domestic woman haunts criticism even today.

2 ❧ VANISHING AMERICANS:

JAMES FENIMORE COOPER

James Fenimore Cooper's *The Last of the Mohicans* is one of approximately forty novels published in the United States between 1824 and 1834 that together suggest the existence of a virtual "cult of the Vanishing American" in the antebellum period. Requisite to membership in this cult was a belief that the rapid decrease in the native population noted by many Jacksonian-era observers was both spontaneous and ineluctable.[1] Cooper would seem to betray his indoctrination in the cult of the Vanishing American when he states in the introduction to the 1831 edition of his novel that it was "the seemingly inevitable fate of all [native tribes]" to "disappear before the advances . . . of civilisation [just] as the verdure of their native forests falls before the nipping frost."[2] The elegiac mode here performs the historical sleight of hand crucial to the topos of the doomed aboriginal: it represents the disappearance of the native not just as natural but as having already happened.[3]

In the novel itself, of course, Cooper's Indians "vanish" in somewhat more spectacular fashion than the introductory invocation of forest and frost leads us to anticipate. However pacific the introduction's simile, in the narrative proper, individual representatives of the "doomed" race expire in utterly sensational ways. Indeed, the frequency with which Cooper's Indians plunge to their deaths from great heights is positively dumbfounding.

The most memorable instance of this is the villainous Magua's spectacular demise at the end of the novel. Evading pursuit by Cooper's white hero Hawk-eye, Magua attempts to leap from the brow of a mountain to an adjacent precipice, but he falls "short of his mark" and finds himself dangling from a "giddy height," clinging desperately to a shrub growing from the side of the precipice. Bent on destroying his enemy, Hawk-eye fires. The wounded Magua's hold loosens, and "his dark person [is] seen cutting the air with its head downwards, for a fleeting instant . . . in its rapid flight to destruction" (338).

To claim that Cooper earlier foreshadows Magua's Miltonic fall would grossly understate the case. Indeed, the fall of dark persons from on high is a virtual theme in *The Last of the Mohicans*. Similar rapid flights to destruction abound, for example, in an early confrontation between whites and enemy Indians that takes place in the vertiginous topography of a huge cavern. One Indian plunges "into [a] deep and yawning abyss" (69). A second hurls "headlong among the clefts of [an] island" (70). A third tumbles down an "irrecoverable precipice" (71), while yet another drops "like lead" into the "foaming waters" below (75).[4]

Mere sensationalism does not quite account for Cooper's fascination with the precipitous dark person. The figure sometimes surfaces in relatively banal forms—for example, when the noble savage Uncas at one point darts "through the air" and lands upon Magua, "driving him many yards . . . headlong and prostrate" (113), or later when, in his fatal attempt to save Cora Munro's life, Uncas leaps between her and Magua in an act that Cooper calls "headlong precipitation" (336). And perhaps the most banal reiteration of the figure occurs when the novelist describes a Huron, tomahawk in his hand and malice in his heart, rushing at Uncas. A quick-witted white man sticks out his foot to trip the "eager savage" as he passes, and the Huron is "precipitated . . . headlong" to the ground (238). Etymologically considered ("precipitation" is from *praeceps* or "headlong"), the phrase is as peculiarly reiterative as the headlong aboriginal it describes.

I would like to suggest that the redundancy of both phrase and figure in Cooper's novel signals that text's participation in and instantiation of a larger antebellum cultural discourse in which the ethnographic and pedagogic overlap. Cooper at one point refers to an enemy Huron who is about to plunge down a precipice as a "prodigy" (69). An educational treatise written by a doctor and appearing six years after *The Last of the Mohicans* discusses the phenomenon of precocity and provides a compelling if unlikely analogue to Cooper's precipitous native. In his *Remarks on the Influence of Mental Cultivation and Mental Excitement Upon Health*, Dr. Amariah Brigham records the case of a white prodigy, one William M., born in Philadelphia on the Fourth of July, 1820. While still a toddler, William M. astonished those around him with his musical talents, his conversational skills, and his lofty moral sentiments.

According to Brigham, "the heads of great thinkers . . . are wonderfully large." At birth William M.'s head "was of ordinary size," but "very soon, after an attack of dropsy of the brain, it began to grow inordinately." Indeed, by the time the child learned to walk, his head had grown so large that "he was apt to fall, especially forwards, from readily losing his equilibrium." This tendency proved to be more than a minor annoyance. At eight years of age he suffered a precipitous demise—a death both untimely and literally headlong. Losing his balance one day, he fell headfirst against a door, bruised his forehead, "became very sick, and died the next evening." William M.'s fatal loss of equilibrium evinces the thesis advanced in this section of Brigham's treatise, namely, that "mental precocity is generally a symptom of disease; and hence those who exhibit it very frequently, die young." A "passion for books" and other mental excitements may, in the doctor's opinion, presage early death.[5]

The ethnographic subtext of Brigham's thesis (and hence the treatise's relevance to Cooper's novel) becomes more legible when William M.'s story is juxtaposed with Margaret Fuller's discussion of equilibrium and race in her account of a journey into Indian territory in *A Summer on the Lakes* (1844). In fact, the case of William M. reads like a curiously materialist interpretation of what Fuller calls "civilized man['s] larger mind." Fuller sees the difference between "civilized" and "savage" as in part a matter of proportions, a difference of relative development of mind and body. Civilized man "is constantly breaking bounds, in proportion as the mental gets the better of the mere instinctive existence." In the process, however, "he loses in harmony of being what he gains in height and extension; the civilized man is a larger mind but a more imperfect nature than the savage." What Fuller calls "civilized man['s] larger mind," Brigham translates into civilized man's larger *head*—but even Fuller's analysis has a materialist component. She asserts that Indian tribes subjugated by whites cease to bear physical resemblance to members of their race who are uncontaminated by civilization. Unlike other natives, members of conquered tribes, she writes, are "no longer strong, tall, or finely proportioned."[6]

Whereas Fuller imagines that physical degeneration in the form of disproportion is desirable because it fosters spiritual development, Brigham believes in "the necessity of giving more attention to the health and growth of the body, and less to the cultivation of the mind . . . than is now given." But Brigham's concern extends beyond individual bodies and their well-being. Educational treatises published in the United States in the antebellum period slide easily from the individual to the race. Brigham's preface declares, "The people of the United States ought to become the most vigorous and powerful race of human beings, both in mind and body, that the world has ever known."[7] William M.'s significant birthplace (Philadelphia) and birthdate (the Fourth of July) render him the local instance of an alleged racial defiance of Brigham's imperialist imperative.

The same entanglement of child-rearing and empire-building surfaces in the work of his contemporary Catharine Beecher—whose popular advice to housewives and whose former position as head of the prestigious Hartford Female Seminary guaranteed her pedagogy both domestic and institutional influence.[8] Like Brigham, Beecher worried that Anglo-American children were "becoming less and less healthful and good-looking" and that they were every year producing children even "more puny and degenerate" than themselves. Beecher contrasts puny Anglo-Americans with the robust ancient Greeks, who, she asserts, were of a stock so vigorous that they "conquered nearly the whole world."[9] This last comment suggests the way in which early-nineteenth-century educational treatises—characteristically if not constitutionally—traverse the discursive registers of home and empire. The figure of the prodigy, one may conclude, organizes into a single discursive economy two distinct cultural arenas expressed through binarisms of feminine and masculine, private and public, suburbia and frontier, sentiment and adventure.[10] Expressing these binarisms in somewhat different terms, I would claim that the prodigy illuminates the affiliations of the micro- and the macro-political.

Genocide and Modernity

Michel Foucault supplies a model for uncovering the connections between micro- and macropolitics when (in anticipating objections to his characterization of modern government as "power organized around the management of life rather than the menace of death")[11] he concedes that the modernity of the genocidal might seem to suggest that the life-destroying power of the sovereign not only survived his decapitation but actually escalated in the nineteenth and twentieth centuries. Conceiving of modern power as the power to administer life rather than the power to inflict death would seem to require ignoring the genocidal animus which has characterized Western interaction with both Jews and people of color in the modern era. By emphasizing production, Foucauldian theory would seem unable to account for the racial holocausts that have punctuated the modern era and hence would seem necessarily to marginalize (if not to erase altogether) an important part of the history of Jews and the Third World.

Yet, even if race remains a largely undeveloped category of analysis in the history it traces, *The History of Sexuality* does theorize interracial conflict as an inevitable component of modernity. Foucault asserts that precisely inasmuch as power legitimates and incarnates itself through "the right of the social body to ensure, maintain, or develop its life," racial holocaust becomes "vital" to its expression. Arguing for the simultaneity of productive technologies that promote the well-being of the individual and deductive technologies that ensure the well-being of the race, he writes that in eighteenth- and nineteenth-century Europe "precocious sexuality was presented . . . as an epidemic menace that risked compromising not only the future health of adults but the future of the entire society and species."[12] Modifying Foucault's analysis slightly, I will be locating antebellum representations of the prodigy—a less explicitly sexualized relative of the precocious child—on the discursive axis of two distinctive forms of power in modern Western societies.

Foucault's remarks on genocide unsettle the thumbnail literary history proposed earlier in *The History of Sexuality*. There Foucault posits that the rise of the micropolitical corresponds roughly with the displacement of narratives of adventure by narratives of sentiment: "we have passed from a pleasure to be recounted . . . centering on the heroic . . . narration of 'trials' of bravery . . . to a literature ordered according to the infinite task of extracting [truth] from the depths of oneself."[13] Perhaps one consequence of this statement is that Foucauldian criticism has concentrated on domestic, realist, and sentimental fictions to the neglect of adventure fictions (which, because they so often unfold on borders between "civilized" and "savage," frequently engage questions of the survival of races). Foucauldian New Historicist critics writing about the nineteenth century—particularly Richard Brodhead, Nancy Armstrong, and D. A. Miller—have constructed the home and its narratives as, in Miller's words, the domain of an "extralegal series of 'micropowers' " and hence the proper sphere for Foucauldian inquiry.[14] But if we take seriously Foucault's comments about the involution of micro- and macropowers around questions of race, then we would expect to uncover not the superannuation of heroism by sentiment but rather their simultaneity and co-implication. The ease with which educational treatises like Beecher's and Brigham's oscillate from the individual to the race suggests the pertinence of Foucauldian analysis to race relations. Similarly, analysis of the figure of the precipitous aboriginal whose precocity signals his "inevitable" demise in *The Last of the Mohicans* suggests that this type of analysis is as relevant to imperial fictions as it is to domestic ones.

This reading of the relation between home and frontier, however, suggests more than the need for simple expansion of the domain of New Historicism. I would like to use this reading as an occasion to interrogate the politics of Foucauldian analysis itself. Uncovering the interaction between micro- and macropolitical concerns raises some questions about the gender and racial politics of the Foucauldian "shift" from which New Historicist criticism on the nineteenth century proceeds. A shift from an economy of punishment to one of discipline is not just passively evidenced but instead actively deployed in early-nineteenth-century U.S. representations of the prodigy.

It is not simply that antebellum texts like *The Last of the Mochicans* either prefigure or preempt contemporary theoretical and critical developments (although I *would* claim that New Historicism of the Foucauldian variety has in its discussion of power recapitulated more than it has analyzed nineteenth-century critiques of domesticity). More importantly, I would argue that a reading of antebellum texts demonstrates that narratives of the shift from punishment to discipline (like the one Foucauldian New Historicism has given us) have, historically, operated to the detriment of both white middle-class women and people of color. Whatever its politics within its own cultural setting, Foucauldian knowledge does not encounter a political vacuum when it enters contemporary U.S. critical discourse. Instead it meets with a history extending back to the antebellum period in which intellectuals have deployed narratives of a shift in the nature of power toward politically suspicious ends. For this reason contemporary intellectuals in the United States whose work has been influenced by Foucault (myself included) need to historicize their own discourse by reconstructing its genealogy and inquiring into the rhetorical work performed by the Foucauldian shift that supplies their work with its hard historical foundations.

Momism and Mohicans

Just as Brigham encodes in William M.'s brief life the ethnographic logic supporting an account of the decline of Anglo-Americans, compacted within Cooper's precipitous aboriginal is a logic ensuring the ideological transformation of Native Americans into Vanishing Americans. Despite the spectacular nature of their individual deaths, Cooper's natives, every bit as much as his introductory reference to the "verdure . . . fall[ing] before the nipping frost," expunge imperialist conflict from the Jacksonian cultural memory. They do so by foregrounding issues of proportion and equilibrium so crucial to antebellum accounts of the so-called disappearance of races.

Cooper incorporates the racial other as an earlier and now irretrievably lost version of the self. Perhaps this is part of the reason why our culture has come to regard *The Last of the Mohicans* and other nineteenth-century Anglo-American frontier fictions as "children's literature." Just as Freud in his essay on "The Sexual Aberrations" collapses the "primitive" or "archaic" and the infantile,[15] Cooper conflates racial difference and temporal distance on an evolutionary continuum of human history. In other words, it is as though for him aboriginals represent a phase that the human race goes through but must inevitably get over. Regardless of whether the ethno-pedagogic text celebrates equilibrium (in the case of Cooper and Brigham) or disequilibrium (in the case of Fuller), in equating the savage and the juvenile it starts by assuming that certain Americans must vanish.

Cooper's concern with proportion registers his debt to ethno-pedagogic thinking. The novel's white characters marvel over the "perfection of form which abounds among the uncorrupted natives" (53), and the narrator himself praises what he calls Uncas's "beautiful proportions" (275). Uncas is "an unblemished specimen of the noblest proportions of man" and resembles "some precious relic of the Grecian chisel" (53). In the Western tradition the ancient Greeks had long represented the ideal of physical beauty, but in the antebellum United States their beautiful proportions had become the sine qua non of a call for educational reform. Beecher, for example, launches her critique of the U.S. educational system with the observation that the Greeks "were remarkable, not only for their wisdom and strength, but for their great beauty, so that the statues they made to resemble their own men and women have, ever since, been regarded as the most perfect forms of human beauty." "Perfect forms" here conveys roughly what "beautiful proportions" connotes in Cooper: a balance of intellectual and physical culture—hence Beecher's interest in the Greek educational system as a model for contemporary times. According to her, the Greeks' perfection of form derived from the fact that "they had two kinds of schools— the one to train the minds, and the other to train the bodies of their children."[16]

Whatever nostalgia Cooper expresses for savage equilibrium in his description of Uncas, he imagines that civilization necessarily spells the end of archaic proportions. Hence he contrasts Uncas's "beautiful proportions" with the white man David Gamut's "rare proportions" (17). Gamut, writes the novelist, possesses "all the bones and joints of other men, without any of their proportions." While Cooper reassures us that Gamut is not actually physically "deformed," his description of Gamut does little to assuage his reader's anxiety on that score:

> His head was large; his shoulders narrow; his arms long and dangling; while his hands were small, if not delicate. His legs and thighs were thin nearly to emaciation, but of extraordinary length; and his knees would have been considered tremendous, had they not been outdone by the broader foundations [i.e., his feet] on which this false superstructure of blended human orders, was so profanely reared. (16)

Gamut's peculiar proportions are just one sign that he is the vehicle by which civilization is carried into the wilderness. Around him also accrue linked images of language, femininity, and power. Referring to Gamut's annoying habit of bursting into song whenever the proximity of enemy Indians demands absolute silence (Gamut is a psalmodist by profession), Hawk-eye laments the fact that, as he puts it, although the "Lord never intended that the man should place all his endeavours in his throat," Gamut had "fallen into the hands of some silly woman, when he should have been gathering his education under a blue sky, and among the beauties of the forest" (224).

While perhaps Cooper, like Hawk-eye, believes that God never intended that man privilege language at the expense of the development of the body, both seem to believe that the Supreme Being intended that *woman* do so. This is suggested by Cooper's habitual association of feminine control over education in the settlements with both the proliferation of words and with precipitous behavior. For example, as darkness begins to settle on his party's search for clues to the whereabouts of the captive Munro sisters, Hawk-eye advises his companions to abandon the trail until morning. "In the morning," he insists, "we shall be fresh, and ready to undertake our work like men, and not like babbling women, or eager boys" (189).

Hawk-eye's association of loquacious femininity and headstrong boys has antecedents in Rousseauvian notions of noble savagery. In *Émile* women's control over the education of children threatens the survival of the white race: "puberty and sexual potency," according to Rousseau, "always arrive earlier in learned and civilized peoples than in ignorant and barbarous peoples," and this explains why Europeans (unlike noble savages) are "exhausted early, remain small, weak, . . . ill-formed" and die young. "Man's weakness," he writes, proceeds from "the inequality between his strength and his desires."[17] Only in boyhood and savagery is there an equilibrium of body (what we can get) and mind (what we want), and for Rousseau equilibrium is synonymous with nobility— a quality whose residual existence boyhood guarantees in civilized societies.

Émile's antifeminism derives from Rousseau's belief that, because their lack of physical strength prevents them from attaining self-sufficiency, women inevitably want more than they can get. The satisfaction of even a woman's most basic wants necessarily requires that she defraud her constitutional destiny by using words to persuade others to do for her what she cannot do for herself. Women, feels Rousseau, must and should rely upon men to get what they want. The problem arises when women are given unsupervised control over the education of boys. Whereas the father can discipline the child through simple physical coercion (which Rousseau heartily recommends), the mother must resort to complex sentimental manipulations expressed in words. Individual pedagogical errors are revenged upon the race as the son discovers that the efficacy of the verbal tool obviates the necessity of bodily vigor. Imitating the mother's example, the boy learns to defraud the body through "feminine" acts of representation, destroys the juvenile balance of needs and strength, and thereby becomes a prodigy. Put in Cooper's terms, in *Émile* babbling women yield eager boys.

Cooper's Rousseauvian subtext emerges when one of his noble savages asserts that "men speak not twice" (314). Real men do not need words because they have physical strength. Women and precocious sons, however, require verbal prosthetics to get what they want. Furthermore, for Cooper as well as for Rousseau, words represent a whole economy of power marked as feminine. Thus, after declaring himself a warrior not a reader, Hawk-eye asserts that he, unlike Gamut, is no "whimpering boy, at the apron string of one of your old gals" (117). Free of books, Hawk-eye liberates himself from the power that nineteenth-century domesticity gave to women—liberates himself from what Leslie Fiedler calls the "gentle tyranny of home and woman."[18] Hence when Gamut demands that Hawk-eye buttress one of his numerous philosophical speculations with some authoritative textual prop, the enraged scout demands, "What have such as I, who am a warrior of the wilderness . . . to do with books! I never read but in one [that is, the book of nature], and the words that are written there are too simple and too plain to need much schooling" (117). I would argue that the fiction of the "plainness" of the book of nature in this passage supports another fiction: that of the legibility of the paternal power imagined as simple physical force. Cooper attempts to differentiate between knowledge gained from experience on the trail and "bookish knowledge" (189) in order to create the fiction of power relations "plain" as nature itself.

Both the disregard for books and the association of them with the newly empowered antebellum woman are staples of the period. Although the book is usually associated with the reign of the father, in the antebellum period *books* seem to be associated with the reign of the mother. The pervasiveness of this association is suggested by Thoreau's chapter "Reading" in *Walden*. There the author expresses his disgust not just over the quality of popular books but also over their quantity. Embedded within Thoreau's anxiety about multiplicity lies an anxiety about the mother's assumption of the educational duties formerly administered by the father—or so Thoreau's confusion of mechanical production and female sexual reproduction leads one to suspect.

Thoreau confuses the printing press with the womb when he derides the "modern cheap and fertile press." Machinelike literary mothers produce not only insubstantial volumes (like the popular series called "Little Reading," which the author came across one day in his local library); they also produce insubstantial people. Thoreau characterizes the readers of "Little Reading" as themselves little, like the "modern puny and degenerate race" described by Beecher. They are "pygmies and manikins" and "a race of tit-men." The author distinguishes this modern race from the archaic, athletic, and robust race of men nurtured by literary fathers before the age of mechanical reproduction. According to "Reading," in a heroic age long past it "require[d] a training such as the athletes underwent" to read literature. Whereas the modern press is "fertile," "the heroic writers of antiquity" produced works which were "solitary."[19]

Thoreau's opposition of the feminine, the diminutive, and the multiple against the masculine, the massive, and the singular services a Rousseauvian distinction between power conceived of as a physical force and power conceived of as verbal and sentimental manipulation. The solidity of the paternal book in "Reading" symbolizes the visibility of power relations under the patriarch, and the robustness of the (male) reader of the (male) classics denotes his ability both to see and to fight whatever threatens his autonomy. Hence Thoreau writes that, even if read in translation (in what he calls "our *mother* tongue") the massive "heroic books" are written in a language alien to the modern reader. They "will always be in a language dead to degenerate times," and therefore they require readers to "laboriously seek the meaning of each word and line." The laboriousness of the reading preserves the autonomy of the subject. The classics speak in a "*father* tongue, a reserved and select expression" that does not compromise volition because, rather than lulling the reader to sleep, it demands that he "devote [his] most alert and wakeful hours" to reading. By contrast, we learn our mother tongue "unconsciously" and hence read popular books like sleepwalkers. In "Reading" the smallness of books written by women suggests not just their trivial contents but also the microscopic scale of maternal power. Thoreau's comment that readers of little books are "machines" anticipates the Foucauldian anxiety over a power whose invisibility (accomplished through domestication, decentering, and proliferation) only augments its efficiency.[20]

Although Thoreau's chapter reads like an attempt to disempower the domestic woman, the same disparaging association of mass-production and female generativity made by Thoreau surfaces even in the texts apparently most instrumental in instituting the reign of the mother. Domestic ideology's demonic double, what Michael Paul Rogin dubs "momism,"[21] is if anything even more evident in the work of Hannah More, the British author generally credited with the founding of domestic ideology. Her influential treatise on female education was reprinted in numerous editions in the U.S. between 1800 and 1826 and helped determine the shape of domesticity in this country as well as in Britain.

In *Strictures on the Modern System of Female Education,* More, like Thoreau, expresses anxiety about the quantity of "little books" on the market. "Real" knowledge and piety, she writes, have suffered from "that profusion of little, amusing, sentimental books with which the youthful library overflows." After questioning the pedagogical value of multiplying the number of books students read, More is overcome by a proto-Malthusian vision of the uncontrollably generative popular press. She writes: "Who are those ever multiplying authors, that with unparalleled fecundity are overstocking the world with their quick-succeeding progeny? They are the novel-writers; the easiness of whose productions is at once the cause of their own fruitfulness, and of the almost infinitely numerous race of imitators, to whom they give birth."[22] More's nightmare vision identifies female sexual reproduction with the mechanical production increasingly characteristic of the book industry. Mass-production of children (the creation of a "race of imitators") is the evil twin of domestic ideology's attempt to standardize child-rearing practices.

The hysteria over the abundance of books in the antebellum period both represents and creates an anxiety over the violation of the independence of the subject by disciplinary methods directed at the interior rather than at the body. An anxiety over the decorporealization of power compels the advice offered time and again in educational treatises in the early nineteenth century: more emphasis should be placed upon the cultivation of the juvenile body and less upon the development of the juvenile mind. The excessively cerebral Anglo-Saxon in More's text stands on the verge of disappearing as power disappears. The Anglo-Saxon race, she writes, is threatened with the same "quick succession of slavery, effeminacy, . . . vice, . . . and degeneracy" that overtook the inhabitants of ancient Rome.[23]

For Cooper, to read in the book of nature is to be educated through the paternal apprenticeship system rather than the maternal representational system. Cooper suggests this when at one point in the narrative Chingachgook and Hawk-eye lose Magua's trail. Uncas, who has long since uncovered the proper path, nevertheless assumes a "calm and dignified demeanour" suggestive of "dependen[ce] on the sagacity and intelligence of the seniors of the party" (213). Savage society, in Cooper as in Rousseau, does not produce prodigies. According to the novelist, when members of Indian tribes convene to confer on matters important to the whole community,

> there is never to be found any impatient aspirant after premature distinction, standing ready to move his auditors to some hasty, and, perhaps, injudicious discussion, in order that his own reputation may be the gainer. An act of so much precipitancy and presumption, would seal the downfall of *precocious* intellect for ever. It rested solely with the oldest and most experienced of the men to lay the subject of the conference before the people. (292, my italics)

Indian society then offers a highly visible version of power. According to the narrator, the power of the Indian leader is the power of physical force: "the authority of an Indian chief [is] so little conventional, that it [is] oftener maintained by physical superiority, than by any moral supremacy he might possess" (92).

If basing power on physical superiority prevents aboriginal precocity, it also makes the patriarch's control over the tribe tenuous. Even Cooper's most noble savages seem barely restrained by the father. Uncas's "dignified and calm demeanor" disappears at a moment's notice. As soon as Chingachgook solicits his help, Uncas bounds "forward like a deer" and directs his elders to the proper trail (213). The young Mohican's sudden shift from rocklike self-restraint to frenetic activity is one that characterizes natives whether represented individually or in groups. Such fluctuations in Indian demeanor suggest what Cooper imagines as the fundamental exteriority to the self of power legitimated by physical superiority. Despite its patriarchal nature, Indian government permits radical independence because, like the authority exercised by Foucault's sovereign, that restraint is imagined to be of a strictly corporeal nature.

Fiedler's "gentle tyranny," on the other hand, would subvert radical native independence and undermine native proportions. This is in fact what happens to Uncas. Aware at some level of Uncas's admiration of her, Cora gains an "intuitive consciousness of her power" over the young Mohican (79). Like the ethnologists of his day Cooper believed Indians experienced no romantic passion.[24] Hence he calls Uncas's enamored ministrations to Cora both a "departure from the dignity of his manhood" and an "utter innovation on . . . Indian customs" (56). His love "elevate[s] him far above the intelligence, and advance[s] him . . . centuries before the practices of his nation" (115).

Cooper seems to imagine that Cora's gentle tyranny "seal[s] the downfall" of Uncas's "precocious intellect." Falling under Cora's power, educated without his knowledge, Uncas dies a racial prodigy. Hawk-eye notes the Mohican's uncharacteristic precipitancy during their search for the captive Munro sisters. He chastises Uncas for suddenly becoming "as impatient as a man in the settlements" (185). The noble savage turned eager savage repeatedly puts himself at risk in pursuing the captive Cora Munro: "In vain Hawk-eye called to him to respect the covers; the young Mohican braved the dangerous fire of his enemies, and soon compelled them to a flight as swift as his own headlong speed" (334).

Significantly, it is this precocious development under woman's invisible tutelage that makes Uncas the *last* of the Mohicans. At the end of the novel, he stands upon a ledge overlooking Magua, who is threatening Cora with a tomahawk. The impassioned Mohican leaps "frantically, from a fearful height" and falls between Magua and his intended target, but only to fall victim himself to Magua's tomahawk (337). Cooper reports Magua's headlong death at Hawk-eye's hands on the very next page of the novel; and the language of precipitancy, the reiteration of the image of the headlong Indian, encourages us to confuse the two red men. Invoking the antebellum figure of the prodigy, Cooper's text replaces Hawk-eye's rifle with the middle-class woman's apron strings.[25] It translates fire power into mother power.

Gender, Empire, and New Historicism

The Last of the Mohicans deflects attention from the macropolitical realm represented in the text by the army (for which Hawk-eye is a scout), and upon women falls the responsibility for the "disappearance" of the native. But the prodigy's presence does more than deflect. The threat that woman's invisible power poses to the male subject produces the need for some space (the frontier) in order to elude her miasmic influence and hence makes imperative the macropolitical controls effecting Indian removal from contiguous territories. In other words Cooper's "discovery" of the discipline deployed against his white men legitimates the technologies of punishment deployed against his red men.

Antebellum discourse, I have argued, uses images of the modern proliferation of words as a sign that feminine words have replaced masculine muscle as the basis of authority. Momist imagery of the loss of autonomy resulting from this feminization of power expresses nostalgia for a form of power whose lack of psychic consequences guarantees that it does not compromise the autonomy of the male subject. Yet neither this subject nor this form of power ever existed. Because it is administered and experienced by human agents, even "simple" brute force must have psychic consequences and must produce subjectivities particular to it.

The fantasy of simple brute force in antebellum discourse generates what Renato Rosaldo calls "imperialist nostalgia." "When the so-called civilizing process destabilizes forms of life," writes Rosaldo, "the agents of change experience transformations of other cultures as if they were personal losses."[26] Developing Rosaldo's point, Amy Kaplan suggests that such nostalgia makes aggression against third world peoples the logical consequence of antifeminism directed against first world women because in it "the empire figures as the site where you can be all that you can no longer be at home—a 'real live man'—where you can recover the autonomy denied by social forces of modernization, often aligned in this way of thinking with feminization."[27]

Following Rosaldo and Kaplan, I would argue that in our own time scholarship on the alleged feminization of society itself participates in the imperialist nostalgia of the discourse it analyzes. Traditionally, momist texts like Cooper's were seen as evidence of a historical "feminization of American culture" in which expanded female leisure and literacy permitted Hawthorne's "scribbling women" to usurp the cultural offices once occupied by less prolific but more profound male authors.[28] More recently, New Historicist criticism of the Foucauldian variety has encouraged us to regard the feminization of culture as a symptom of a larger feminization of power. Yet, the novelty of New Historicism does not reside in its emphasis on power. Earlier cultural analysis also equated feminization with normalization. Richard Brodhead's recent characterization of the modern ideal of maternal love as a power whose "silken threads are harder to burst than the iron chains of authority" employed by "old-style paternal force" recalls Fiedler's analysis of the rise of a "gentle tyranny of home and woman" in the nineteenth century.[29] D. A. Miller's revelation of a nineteenth-century "field of power relations" masquerading as a "domesticating pedagogy" harkens back to Ann Douglas's discussion of the "manifold possibilities" offered by Victorian maternal influence for "devious social control."[30] Nancy Armstrong's assertion that domestic ideology provided the "logic" that permitted women to enter the world of work through social services and thereby extended "subtle techniques of domestic surveillance beyond the middle-class home and into the lives of those much lower down on the economic ladder" mirrors Christopher Lasch's claim that "rise of the 'helping professions' " in the early twentieth century allowed "society in the guise of a 'nurturing mother' [to invade] the family, the stronghold of . . . private rights."[31]

Neither the poststructuralist upheaval that divides the cultural analysis of the 1960s and 1970s from that of the 1980s and 1990s nor the feminist critiques to which these analyses have been subjected have altered the basic narrative: normalization is still women's work. What is even more startling is that this narrative appears to date back to antebellum times. Yet, the failure of New Historicists to articulate a genuinely novel reading of the nineteenth century troubles me far less than their apparent obliviousness to the rhetorical content of what they present as historical facts.[32] Even if exposing the rhetorical work of Foucauldian history does not *in and of itself* undermine the facticity of New Historicist claims (all facts require human interpreters and so all truth is necessarily rhetorical), still its practitioners cannot possibly hope to direct their own rhetoric toward progressive ends without first inquiring into the gender and race politics perpetuated by their use of Foucauldian knowledge.[33]

New Historicists' dependence upon Foucault's narrative of modernization would seem to account for their apparent obliviousness to the way in which they have been engaged in the retelling of a politically suspect nineteenth-century narrative of modernization. Despite the emphasis I have put on it, Foucault's assertion that the West's commitment to managing the life of its own population also entails a commitment to massive destruction of populations designated as "other" is parenthetical to the history outlined in the first volume of *The History of Sexuality*. Whereas his brief comments on modern racial holocausts suggest the simultaneity of deductive and productive manifestations of power, Foucault's larger historical narrative (as represented by both *The History of Sexuality* and *Discipline and Punish*) is founded upon a temporal distinction between them such that the deductive (punishment) represents the pre-modern and the productive (discipline) the modern form of power. Hence Foucault's own narrative is subject to the same critique to which I have subjected antebellum narratives of modernization. Inasmuch as he defines modernity as the decorporealization of power, he participates in the construction of an utterly mythic time in which authority meant simple physical superiority (an era personified in *Émile* by the father who governs by means of the lash). Foucault's temporalization of the difference between discipline and punishment suggests that even contemporary images of modernity collaborate in the production of the imperialist nostalgia I have been describing.

3 BLACK NATIONALIST HOUSEKEEPING: MARIA W. STEWART

"Suffer me . . . to express my sentiments but this once, however severe they may appear to be, and then hereafter let me sink into oblivion, and let my name die in forgetfulness."
—Maria W. Stewart, *Productions*[1]

A number of critics have discussed ex-slave Frederick Douglass's physical standoff with his overseer Covey as a condensation of the gendered subtext of nineteenth-century African American nationalism.[2] This chapter engages these critics through a consideration of the writings of Maria W. Stewart, an abolitionist speaker active in the 1830s who apparently was hounded off the podium because of her controversial promotion of women's right to full citizenship in the black nation imagined by Douglass and other male writers and orators.[3] Like the previous chapter, this one demonstrates the gendered languages of oppositionality arising from the discursive exchange between the domestic ideologues and their critics—this time in the context of a budding social movement that (until the 1840s) operated largely outside of the Anglo-American, middle-class cultural infrastructure.[4]

In Eric J. Sundquist's book *To Wake the Nations,* the paradigm of violent, redeeming struggle inherited from the American Revolution dictates the signs of black masculinist resistance. "In this celebrated scene," writes Sundquist,

> Douglass accentuates his own conversion to mastery—mastery of Covey, in a reversal of the relationship of power, and mastery of himself, in a release from the condition of chattelism. A "boy of sixteen," Douglass has vanquished his master, assumed his

place psychologically, and fathered himself in the dramatic act of resistance. . . .

[T]hough he is still in the physical chains of slavery . . . [by the end of the scene, Douglass] stands . . . arrayed in masculine liberty, endowed with the "signs of power."[5]

According to Sundquist, Douglass's reoccupation of the ideology of the founding fathers makes his autobiography "archetypal[ly] American" as well as "archetypal[ly] *black* American." *My Bondage and My Freedom* translates slave insurrection "across the color line," making possible the integration of African American insurgency into an already available Anglo-American national history by imaging the former as the "completion of the stymied Revolution of 1776" (a revolution which had failed so conspicuously to found a state that treated all men as created equal).[6]

If, as Sundquist argues so persuasively, Douglass's physical mastery of Covey symbolically constitutes him as "a son of the Revolution" and part of the American "family of liberty," one wonders what vocabulary antebellum African American women had for articulating the presence they desired in this complex national household. The ideology of the American Revolution may translate across the color line; however, given that the color line is really a double line (the double line of color and gender), how would an African American woman—committed equally to both black nationalism and women's participation in that enterprise— make her resistance recognizable?[7]

The initial sections of this chapter attempt to answer this question by reference to Stewart's remarkable but underanalyzed polemics against slavery and racism through which she expounded black nationalist objectives.[8] The free-born Stewart addressed African American audiences in Boston, Massachusetts, between 1831 and 1833. There she had evidently cultivated connections with a flourishing and largely independent black activist community.[9] When both her friend David Walker and her husband died within a few months of each other, Stewart's grief seems to have triggered first a spiritual crisis and then her formal conversion to Christianity.[10] Sustained by a conviction that God sometimes selects humble vessels to perform sacred missions, Stewart launched a short-lived speaking career which blended millenialist jeremiad with secular nationalism. William Lloyd Garrison's newspaper *The Liberator* printed the speeches as they appeared. In 1835 Stewart collected and published them under the title, *Productions of Mrs. Maria W. Stewart.* They have been available in a modern edition since 1987.

Stewart's writings do indeed provide an answer to my query about the gendered idioms of African American aspiration; however, their ultimate significance for my purposes resides in what they—and their equally important erasure from the black nationalist consciousness— reveal about how the deployment of gender as a sign of oppositionality limits the egalitarian politics expressed in domestic ideology as much as in nineteenth-century black nationalism. Given critics' analysis of Douglass, Stewart's exile from the African American nationalist memory is less surprising when framed as evidence of masculinist bias than when thought of as an expatriation mandated by Stewart's own effort to use a politicized version of domesticity to license her intrusion into a male-dominated arena. Moreover, I believe there is reason to speculate that, if Stewart's name has "die[d] in forgetfulness," womanist as well as masculinist politics conspired in sealing that fate.

Signs of Nationalism

The scant discussion of African American women in Sundquist's study and his complete omission of any reference to Stewart suggests the degree of difficulty involved in rendering women's presence in nationalist movements audible. Although *To Wake the Nations* includes a brief section on African American novelist Pauline Hopkins, its location at the end of his book resonates inauspiciously with Sundquist's revolutionary paradigm: Hopkins, belated in appearance, cannot figure as one of the founding fathers of black America. In Sundquist's study, Douglass, David Walker, Nat Turner, Martin Delany, Charles Chesnutt, and W. E. B. DuBois (and more obscure men like Robert Alexander, with oeuvres even less substantial than Stewart's) have prior claims on the patronymic. Moreover, if Hopkins introduced the "woman question" into black nationalist discourse so belatedly, that question would appear supplementary rather than constitutive, a dream deferrable until the "real" battle is won.

Black female belatedness is by no means unique to Sundquist's discussion of African American nationalism. His book follows historian Wilson Jeremiah Moses's precedent in *The Golden Age of Black Nationalism* by in effect dating women's entrance into black nationalism to the turn of the century.[11] Even the recent Schomburg Library republication of Stewart's writings fails to acknowledge her work in founding the black national household; it packages her as the stepchild of Teresa of Avila (as opposed to sister to Nat Turner) when it identifies her, not as a nationalist but rather as the practitioner of a more properly "feminine" tradition: the spiritual narrative.[12]

With respect to gender, contemporary cultural historiography honors precedents set by nationalist movements themselves. Political scientist Cynthia Enloe observes that (like their official equivalents) insurgent[13] "nationalism[s] typically [have] sprung from masculinized memory, masculinized humiliation and masculinized hope." Eighteenth- and nineteenth-century bourgeois Anglo-European colonists rebelled against what they perceived as the metropolis's insult to their collective "manhood." But "[a]nger at being 'emasculated' " has also driven nineteenth- and twentieth-century nationalisms among indigenous populations dispossessed and dispersed by Anglo-European imperialism and colonialism.[14]

Despite the scarce reference to Stewart in histories of black nationalism, there are unmistakable ideological congruities between her writings and those of other early black nationalists. Like the antebellum figures paid tribute by Sundquist and Moses, Stewart encouraged her audience to understand black racial destiny along the model of the modern nation-state. "All the nations of the earth are crying out for Liberty and Equality" (4). Why, she demanded to know, should African Americans stand alone among "all the nations of the earth" for having failed to "[distinguish] themselves"? (60). Encouraging African Americans to take their inspiration from liberatory movements in France, Greece, Poland, Hungary, Ireland, Haiti—as well as the United States— she advised her audience that blacks would never achieve freedom and equality unless they became an identifiable political collectivity.

Stewart's use of the Anglo-European invaders of North America as role models for the founding of an African American nation-state discloses the sometimes perplexing mix of separatism and identification that characterizes insurgent movements as a result of cultural hybridism; Sundquist notes comparable patterns of dissonance in the work of black male writers throughout the nineteenth century. "Nation-ness is the most universally legitimate value in the political life of our time," writes Benedict Anderson. The editors of *Nationalisms & Sexualities* explain in the introduction to their book of essays that, because of this universal legitimacy, "disenfranchised groups frequently have had to appeal to national values" in order to make their agitation recognizable as a political movement.[15]

Typically, however, eighteenth- and nineteenth-century Anglo-European nationalisms posed territorial solutions to problems of social injustice. Black nationalism in the United States has not always involved geographical separatism. Frustration over the passage of the Fugitive Slave Act of 1850 would kindle black abolitionist interest in territorial solutions, but early black nationalism more often advanced a plan for "racial unity" rather than a literal homeland. Moses writes:

> Black nationalism has sometimes, but not always, been concerned with the quest for a nation in the geographical sense. But often it has been "nationalism" only in the sense that it seeks to unite the entire black racial family, assuming that the entire race has a collective destiny and message for humanity comparable to that of a nation.[16]

The abolitionist context in which autonomous black political organizing arose, in fact, made arguments on behalf of territorial solutions appear ill-advised. Previously, the antislavery movement had drawn its membership from the ranks of wealthy white men, from both North and South. These early antislavery men proposed a two-part solution to the problem of slavery: gradual emancipation secured through the cooperation of slave holders (who would receive financial compensation for their loss) and deportation of all free blacks to Africa (to colonize and "morally uplift that 'heathen' continent"). The formation by these whites of the American Colonization Society in 1816, helped galvanize free blacks into forming their own abolitionist organizations. And these societies vehemently denounced emigration, whether forced or voluntary.[17]

Anti-emigration arguments took a number of forms. "We are *natives* of this country . . ." reasoned one black orator. "Not a few of our fathers suffered and bled to purchase its independence. . . ."[18] Some argued that emancipation would never come if free black agitators left the country. Others opposed colonization on the grounds that its proponents were motivated primarily by racial prejudice (some white antislavery men were themselves slave holders or people who feared miscegenation or believed blacks incapable of the self-reliance a democratic society requires of its citizenry). Others emphasized economic justice. Slave labor, David Walker wrote, had helped make whites rich, and African Americans deserved to benefit from the capital they had generated.[19]

Like Walker, Stewart believed that blacks had the right to enjoy the wealth that "the blood of our fathers, and the tears of our brethren" had netted Anglo-Americans (20). In blunt language, she reminded her audience of the imperialist legacy of the United States and the economic injustice inflicted upon blacks:

> The unfriendly whites first drove the native American from his much loved home. Then they stole our fathers from their peaceful and quiet dwellings, and brought them hither, and made bond-men and bond-women of them and their little ones. . . . [N]ow that we have enriched their soil, and filled their coffers, they say that we are not capable of becoming like white men, and that we can never rise to respectability in this country. They would drive us to a strange land. But before I go, the bayonet shall pierce me through. (71–2)

Even if Stewart considered Africa "a strange land," like other nationalists she imagined that blacks' African origins made them culturally and spiritually distinct from Anglo-Americans. A nascent Pan-Africanist, she represented African Americans as part of a larger, diasporic culture, the scattered remnant of a once-great Ethiopia, humbled for its pride but destined to rise again in the territorial United States:

> History informs us that we sprung from one of the most learned nations of the whole earth; from the seat, if not the parent of science; yes, a poor despised Africa was once the resort of sages and legislators of other nations, was esteemed the school for learning, and the most illustrious men in Greece flocked thither for instruction. But it was our gross sins and abominations that provoked the Almighty to frown thus heavily upon us, and give our glory unto others. Sin and prodigality have caused the downfall of nations. . . . [W]e might . . . despair; but a promise is left us; "Ethiopia shall again stretch forth her hands unto God." (65)

In the context of an antislavery culture dominated by white colonizationist schemes, one can see why the semimythical kingdom of ancient

Ethiopia might seem like a better imaginative location for a black home-land than modern Africa; indeed, other nationalist writers often shared Stewart's mystic vision.[20]

So far I have argued that Stewart's work is comparable to other early-nineteenth-century statements of black nationalism by virtue of its Ethi-opianism, its rejection of geographic separatism, and its hybrid con-struction of a first-person plural on the model of Anglo-European nation-states.[21] But Stewart's nationalist grammar distinguishes itself from that of her antebellum cohort by the particular emphasis it brings to bear on women's role in the creation of a black nation.

Evidently, others in Stewart's community had little to say on the topic of women's participation in the nationalist project. "On my arrival here," she wrote (presumably of her move to Boston),

> [I found] scarce an individual who felt interested in these subjects, and but few of the whites, except Mr. Garrison, and his friend Mr. [Isaac] Knapp; and hearing that those gentlemen had observed that female influence was powerful, my soul became fired with holy zeal . . . (74)

Importantly, the only substantive reference made to an African American woman in *David Walker's Appeal* solicits distrust. Walker re-lates an incident involving a group of slaves who tried to make a break for freedom. Their revolt might have succeeded had it not been for the intervention of a slave woman who resuscitated the overseer they had incapacitated. Concluding his story, Walker raged:

> Was it the natural *fine feelings* of this woman, to save such a wretch alive? . . . For my own part, I cannot think it was any thing but servile deceit, combined with . . . gross ignorance: for we must remember that *humanity, kindness* and the *fear of the Lord,* does not consist in protecting *devils* . . . Ought they not to be destroyed?[22]

Clearly, Walker did not consider race treason a tendency peculiar to women; his *Appeal* provides examples of black male acts of betrayal. But his sarcastic allusion to the slave woman's "natural *fine feelings,*" her "feminine" sentiments, does cast a shadow of suspicion on woman qua woman.

Contemporary political theorist Carole Pateman confronts this shadow in a different context, but her analysis nevertheless elucidates both the dimensions of Walker's suspicion and the character of Stewart's response. Liberal political theory, Pateman writes, divides the world into (on the one hand) a public and masculine sphere of abstract rights and (on the other hand) a private and feminine sphere of affective bonds. Women's political disenfranchisement in the nineteenth century in part depended upon the idea that because women are uniquely adept at experiencing familial and romantic "love," they are as a consequence incapable of exercising the impartial "justice" required of citizens.[23] In Walker's admonitory anecdote, the sentimental weakness associated with women conveys this same skepticism about their capacity to execute justice—and hence voices doubt about African American women's aptitude for citizenship.

Perhaps as a corrective to Walker's representation of African American women as national liabilities, Stewart explicitly demanded women's political inclusion. She supplemented her own example with pronouncements such as ". . . God at this eventful period [has raised] up your . . . females to strive, by their example both in public and private, to assist those who are endeavoring to stop . . . prejudice" (76–7). Old Testament figures like Deborah and Esther, she believed, supported her conviction that women should assume leadership roles. St. Paul may have "declared that it was a shame for a woman to speak in public," but he had no knowledge of the "wrongs and deprivations" modern African Americans faced. Had he foreseen contemporary circumstances, "he would make no objections to [black women's] pleading in public for our rights" (75).

Furthermore, Stewart refuted the charge implied by Walker's anecdote (and endemic to fraternal nationalisms more generally) that women's sentimental natures sabotage their patriotism. In her list of women throughout history who have taken on leadership roles, she includes European "girls" in the fifteenth century who she claims "had studied Eloquence, [and who] would with the sweetest countenances . . . exhort the Pope and the Christian Princes, to declare war against the Turks" (77). "I am as willing to die by the sword as by the pestilence" (53), Stewart declared, imagining violent reprisals on black abolitionists and designating her efforts on behalf of fellow African Americans as "Christian warfare" (79):

[God] hath clothed my face with steel, and lined my forehead with brass. He hath put his testimony within me, and engraven his seal on my forhead [*sic*]. And with these weapons I have indeed set the fiends of earth and hell at defiance. (*75*)

If, as Pateman argues, "nationality, in the last resort, is [thought to be] tested by fighting" and "[a] man's nation is [thought to be] the nation for which he will fight," then Stewart's eagerness to dress womanhood in the wardrobe of battle represents an attempt to redesign women as proper citizens in the era of the modern nation-state.[24]

Douglass offered violence as a threshold for citizenship in his 1863 editorial "Men of Color, To Arms!" There he argued that black men's joining the Union Army was the best way to prove their equality with whites and their status as "Americans."[25] Benedict Anderson also places physical struggle at the definitional core of a range of official and insurgent nationalist movements when he writes in the introduction to *Imagined Communities:* "The central problem posed by nationalism" is explaining how an entity so novel and so artificial could generate such feelings of "deep horizontal comradeship" that "many millions of people" would be willing not just to "kill" but to "die" for it.[26]

By contrast with Douglass's more secular politics, Stewart's biblical language might seem to dilute the evidence of her willingness to embrace the violence both nineteenth- and twentieth-century writers have located at the heart of nationalism; however, one must recall that at the same time that Stewart began ascending the podium in Boston Nat Turner was leading his bloody revolt in Virginia under the mantle of Christian warfare. In an era of hypersensitivity to the threat of black on white violence at home and abroad, references in Stewart to the "many powerful sons and daughters of Africa" prepared to demand "their rights" and, if refused, willing to spread "horror and devastation" (*71*) make her speeches only slightly less incendiary than *David Walker's Appeal.* Nor is the warfare Stewart invoked easily dismissed as mere millennialist metaphor. Walker's mysterious death (probably at the hands of angry slave holders or their agents)[27] and other instances of white on black violence in the North would have made the danger to black activists palpable, even when mediated through biblical paradigms.

Granted, Stewart several times renounces violence as a means of righting racial injustice—but then similar moments of ambivalence towards violence also surface in Douglass's work.[28] In any case, one cannot withhold the descriptive, "nationalist," simply for want of evidence that Stewart actually punched somebody. Sundquist makes it clear that the "redeeming struggle" invoked by Douglass and other black male nationalist intellectuals is a *discursive* production; he attributes to these writers the *signs* of power.

Ethiopia's Mother

Stewart's final address to black Boston (a speech delivered one year before she permanently left that city) indicates that her efforts to represent herself as a proper citizen for a nation recognized through signs of violence failed. "I have made myself contemptible in the eyes of many" (81), she confessed, at the same time that she announced her retirement from public life. But Stewart did not depart without rebuking "enemies" within Boston's black activist community who had "despitefully used and persecuted" her (82). If African Americans continued to "ridicule" the efforts of their "own females" on behalf of abolition and civil rights, "it will be counted for sin" (77). "Let us no longer talk of prejudice, till prejudice becomes extinct at home," she warned. "Let us no longer talk of opposition, till we cease to oppose our own" (78–9).

Both Stewart's abbreviated career in Boston's African American abolitionist community and her virtual disappearance from twentieth-century histories of black nationalism compel one to ask (as a number of scholars have recently asked), "Why is it that the advent of the politics of nationalism signals the subordination if not the demise of women's politics?"[29]

Enloe helps by describing nationalism as "a tool for explaining how inequities have been created between 'us' and 'them.'"[30] Within the nationalist consciousness of "us" and "them" (an opposition that the Douglass/Covey standoff conveys very neatly), one should expect to find internal dissidents made into exiles. Douglass intimates as much when he, otherwise a vocal advocate of gender equality, describes women's rights as a "minor question" and "a side issue" capable of "ren[ding] asunder" the "grand philanthropic movement" of abolitionism.[31] Stewart confounded the meaning of "us" and "them" by naming inequities internal to the African American nation, and in the process she jeopardized the symmetry of the oppressor/oppressed model of political power that Douglass rendered iconic.

While Enloe's approach clarifies the challenge posed to the black nationalist agenda by Stewart's work, differences between the twentieth-century feminism that Enloe scrutinizes and Stewart's antebellum "womanism" merit specification. Enloe notes that contemporary nationalisms have ceded space to female activists inasmuch as the latter have operated under the rubric of "nurturing mother[s]" to the nation.[32] In this sense, and despite the vehemence with which Stewart protested gender oppression within her community, her version of women's rights would have had a less disjunctive effect than contemporary feminism exercises in relation to twentieth-century nationalist movements.

Despite the fact that her vocation as a public lecturer tested the limits of domestic womanhood, Stewart repeatedly invoked and embraced its norms, insisting, for example, that black women's "forms [are] as delicate, and [their] constitutions as slender" as that of their "fairer," middle-class "sisters" (54–5); advising African American women to "strive to excel in good housewifery, knowing that prudence and economy are the road to wealth" (16); and urging them to become "chaste, keepers at home, not busy bodies, meddlers in other men's matters" (10). She also added,

> The [white] American ladies have the honor conferred on them, that by prudence and economy in their domestic concerns, and their unwearied attention in forming the minds and manners of their children, they laid the foundation of their becoming what they now are. (15)

Furthermore, Stewart voiced willingness, even desire, to abdicate the platform, depicting women's public advocacy (in her comments about St. Paul, for example) as a kind of crisis intervention. In casting the contemporary situation as historically anomalous, Stewart's own discursive economy (not just the enmity she apparently aroused in her community) necessitated her eventual erasure. Thus Stewart, well *before* her farewell address, repeatedly staged her death into "forgetfulness": "God will surely raise up those among us who will plead the cause of virtue, and the pure principles of morality, more eloquently than I am able to do" (70–1).

Obviously, domesticity for Stewart did not mean being "compelled to bury [one's mind] and talents beneath a load of iron pots and kettles" (16); to the contrary, this was the situation which she thought that the gendered / racial division of labor had forced on African American women: "look at many of the most worthy and interesting of us [women] doomed to spend our lives in gentlemen's kitchens" (55). Stewart's version of domesticity seems rather to have consisted of what Eileen Boris calls African American "social housekeeping," a kind of activism that "emphasized the role of women as saviors of the race, justifying their [political] activity because they were mothers."[33]

As in Anglo-American domestic ideology, black nationalist social housekeeping blooms from confidence in the moral superiority of womankind. Hence Stewart affirms in one of her speeches that human welfare "almost entirely depends" upon woman's "exertions" (62). The claim requires the correlative construction of male moral evisceration made familiar by domestic ideology, which Stewart also supplied: "Had those men among us, who have had an opportunity, turned their attention as assiduously to mental and moral improvement as they have to gambling and dancing, I might have remained quietly at home, and they stood contending in my place" (67).

Unlike African American women who wrote slave narratives, Stewart did not need to feign adherence to the gender expectations of white patrons and mentors. She addressed audiences composed primarily of other African Americans, and, as Marilyn Richardson notes, "Stewart's initial political arguments grew out of a black protest and abolitionist tradition independent of the later white and integrated organizations which went on to advance the cause of New England abolitionism."[34] Perhaps instead Stewart's domesticity was a facade thrown up to satisfy the gender criteria of an African American rather than Anglo-American audience.[35] If this was the case, however, she seems to have miscalculated either her own rhetorical skill or the perspicacity of her audience or both. Rather than seeing Stewart as a victim of miscalculation, I would argue that she found Anglo-American domestic ideology appealing because it provided a model for writing women into the leadership of nationalist movements.

From her earliest articulation to her midcentury consolidation, the domestic woman has been the "mother" to "America." Republican motherhood, as described in chapter 1, invested the welfare of the nation in women. They became responsible not just for producing and nurturing the bodies of the populace but also for educating impressionable children against corrupting influences which could make them, later in life, unable to perform either masculine political duties or feminine social reproduction. In the antebellum period, women's charge increasingly involved a more abstract body politic which Catharine Beecher called interchangeably the "nation" or the "race." The revaluation of women accomplished by domestic ideology played upon a larger cultural prejudice that God had chosen the United States as his example to the world, the same prejudice used (as Sacvan Bercovitch points out) to justify expansionism as a manifest and sacred national destiny. If, as Beecher wrote, "This is the Country which the Disposer of events designs shall go forth as the cynosure of nations," then (as she also wrote) "to American women . . . is committed the exalted privilege of extending over the world those blessed influences, which are to renovate degraded man."[36]

The co-articulation of Anglo-American nationalism and women's rights in domesticity suspended the privacy of womanhood. It represents a way of figuring citizenship for a population imagined as too mired in personal, affective, and local bonds to participate in an abstract national identity. Stewart's authoritative insertion of herself into the discourse of black male nationalism profited from the claim, made tenable by the intersection of domesticity with nationalism, that women could create a new global order (or rather, that they would *have to* since men, clearly, could not be entrusted with such a precious, moral task).

Given Beecher's endorsement of expansionism, Anglo-American domesticity is an unlikely inspiration for Stewart. And yet casting the United States in the role of exemplary nation did not prevent her from enumerating its transgressions at home and abroad. In fact, taking for granted the exemplary status of the United States gives her critique of white supremacy forcefulness and urgency. If the United States were the location chosen for a divine drama of human regeneration, then whites deserved whatever punishment they had coming to them for so grossly betraying their national mandate. As Stewart would have it:

> . . . America has become like the great city of Babylon. . . . She is
> indeed a seller of slaves and souls of men; . . . her right hand
> supports the reins of government, and her left hand the wheel of

power, and she is determined not to let go her grasp. . . . I believe
that the oppression of injured Africa has come up before the Majesty
of Heaven; and when our cries shall have reached the ears of the
Most High, it will be a tremendous day for the people of this land;
for strong is the arm of the Lord God Almighty. (7 1)

Life and Death in Nationalism

If Stewart has disappeared from view, perhaps it is because her womanist
idiom of social housekeeping does not enjoy the same degree of political
intelligibility that Douglass's masculinist vocabulary commands. From
Douglass's autobiography, one might conclude that the image of the
heroic slave deters recognition of female participation in the nationalist
project by making physical confrontation the definitive expression of
black citizenship. Death and violence in Douglass's work and other
nationalist discourses function as a constellation of signs through which a
certain kind of political subjectivity (national identity) is imaginatively
constituted. Critic Claudia Tate describes the nationalist content of late-
nineteenth century "domestic allegories of political desire" as inaudible
to an ear trained to a masculinist pitch. Such a problem may apply to
Stewart's work as well.

Such a thesis, however, would not explain why at least passages from
Stewart's *Productions* that appear accessible to readers versed in masculinist codes of insurgency (like the last one quoted above) have not been
integrated into cultural histories of black nationalism. Stewart's fear and
fearlessness about her own physical safety, her references to armed
revolt, and her millennialist militancy would seem at least as available to
nationalist recapture as, for example, the narrative of slave Margaret
Garner, the mother who killed her own child to protect her from a life
of enslavement.

I mention Garner's story because of the use Paul Gilroy makes of it in
reading Frederick Douglass's autobiography in *The Black Atlantic*. After
arguing that the Douglass/Covey standoff is "an interesting though
distinctly masculinist resolution of slavery's inner oppositions," Gilroy
nevertheless cites Garner's story in his rebuttal of the thesis that signs of
violence can really serve as "a symptom of important differences in the
philosophical and strategic orientations of black men and women."
Gilroy finds in Garner evidence that black women's and black men's

cultural traditions stand united in renunciation of Western rationality as expressed in the will to live at any cost. In choosing injury and potential freedom over safety and perpetual servitude, both Garner and Douglass "[articulate] a principle of negativity that is opposed to the formal logic and rational calculation characteristic of modern western thinking . . ."[37] Stewart seems to announce a similar "principle of negativity" when she writes (for example): "such is the horrible idea that I entertain respecting a life of servitude, that if I conceived of there being no possibility of my rising above the condition of a servant, I would gladly hail death as a welcome messenger" (53).

Garner's story leads Gilroy to commemorate women's contribution to the origins of black nationalism, but if, as I would argue, the binarism of life and death in nationalist discourse already implies the binarism of female and male, then Gilroy succeeds in ungendering nationalism only at the most literal level. African American women gain entrance into Gilroy's cultural history only by forsaking domesticity, which is to say, by forsaking a discourse about the management and maximumization of life. Gilroy ignores the cognitive dissonance conveyed in Garner's story: as a tale of the perversion of human relations inflicted by the institution of slavery, the narrative of a slave mother killing her own child derives its forcefulness in part from the conventionality of the association of women with nurturing and against death.

The "inclination towards death . . . is fundamental" to Gilroy's definition of nationalism, as it seems to be to contemporary political theorists and cultural historians from Benedict Anderson to Eric J. Sundquist.[38] But nationalism (whether insurgent or official) is a discourse about life as much as about death. The moment of founding the nation expresses itself as the exaction of revolutionary justice; therefore, it speaks the language of death and violence. The quotidian responsibilities of nation building, on the other hand, involve processes of nurturing, education, and social reproduction; therefore, they speak the language of life. Nationalism organizes itself around a gendered division of labor between the task of founding the nation and the task of guaranteeing its posterity—even if these activities are never wholly distinct or necessarily diachronic in their performance.[39] The privileging of the nationalist idiom of violence suggests an unevenness in the recognition of nationalism's different chores.

Significantly, Frederick Douglass himself contributed to this figurative division of labor in his statements in support of women's suffrage. He wrote in his *Life and Times* that

> War, slavery, injustice, and oppression, and the idea that might makes right have been uppermost in all such [male] governments. The slayers of thousands have been exalted into heroes, and the worship of mere physical force has been considered glorious. . . . [M]any reasons can be given to show that woman's influence would greatly tend to check and modify this barbarous and destructive tendency.[40]

If it is represented at all, women's labor on behalf of nationalist causes must appear belated because no matter when women actually perform the labor of the nation, their work is conceived of as the refining touch of modernity upon a more primary act of male definitional violence.

If death is usually understood as black nationalism's native tongue, then Tate's work helps make the dialect of life audible in oppositional political discourse. She argues in her study of Victorian-era writers / activists that "idealized domesticity" is "a fundamental cultural symbol . . . for representing civil ambition . . . a symbol that black women writers in particular used to promote the social advancement of African Americans."[41] Critics' tendency to regard domesticity as the quintessential marker of mindless capitulation rather than as a symbolic system compatible with a range of political positions has prevented them from reading the relation between black women's domestic fiction and black activism. The middle-class values (hard work, education, Christian morality, economy, child-rearing) expressed in Stewart foreshadow the sign system of late-nineteenth-century women writers that leads Houston Baker to characterize their work as "an essentially conservative appeal to white public opinion" and "Victorian morality in whiteface."[42]

The crucial point about Stewart, however, is that she is just as difficult to map onto *womanist* interpretive paradigms of political discourse as she is onto *masculinist* ones. Her career anticipates those of the late-nineteenth-century women writers Tate discusses, but none of them appear to have ever mentioned Stewart's name—despite the fact that they often paid tribute to their literary and political foremothers and despite the fact that Stewart republished her speeches in 1879 and (after giving up lecturing) remained active in black communities outside of Boston until her death that same year.

I would speculate that what really makes Stewart so disruptive to memories of African American political endeavor (whether told from a masculinist or womanist perspective) is the conjunction in her writing of both vocabularies of nationalism: the language of life and the language of death. Stewart's bilingualism threatens not only gender difference but also gender difference as a means of signifying oppositionality. And, although her eccentricity makes her difficult to map onto either masculinist or womanist African American traditions, Stewart remains indispensable for understanding the mutually dependent rhetorics of gender and resistance in the nineteenth century.

Taking the tradition exemplified in Douglass first, one could say that antebellum nationalist manhood states its utopian negation of the status quo through the language of death. In Gilroy's words, Douglass's signs of violence express "a principle of negativity," a wholesale denunciation of "the modern Western consciousness." In such a reading complete negation is the only relation a true nationalism can have to the dominant culture. If one understands nationalism as fundamentally a "principle of negativity," then the *lapse* into the quotidian idiom of life marks a moment when insurgent confuses itself with official, when one is no longer *against* something but *for* something, when one has to announce one's involvement in the messy chores of education, social reproduction, and the interpellation of subjects into citizens: in short, the women's work called bourgeois, assimilationist, even treasonous when enacted by the late-nineteenth-century women writers that Tate revives. Violence in black masculinist discourse guarantees political purity because it is so easily read as a radical break, as pure obliteration of the dominant order. But this radical break must always elude insurgent nationalisms because they depend on official imaginative constructions of the nation and (as Douglass's narrative suggests) their signs of violence are symptoms of black male interpellation into the oedipal order.

The language of masculinity constitutes one trope of resistance in nationalism; the language of life constitutes a second. Women could intrude into matters of government only because their domestic associations retained in the rhetoric of social housekeeping provided a utopian alternative to a putatively male sphere of brute force. The domestic woman could and did leave the home, but she could not do so if she abandoned the claim of her moral difference from men. Stewart repeatedly and flagrantly risks that moral difference by placing sword, shield,

and helmet on the woman warrior. In satisfying the imaginative require-
ments of fraternal nationalism, she forfeits nineteenth-century woman's
only mechanism for justifying their entrance into the political arena.
Thus, late-nineteenth-century African American women intellectuals/
activists simply had to forget Stewart, whose bilingualism threatens the
ground of powerlessness on which social housekeeping rests.

Stewart speaks both masculinist and womanist languages of black
nationalism. Refusing to honor the gendered division of labor, representing herself as both maternal and militant, she voices connections
between violence and nurture. Even when nationalism acknowledges
women as the mothers of the nation, it disjoins violence and nurture
through figures of gender difference. Although deployed differently in
masculinist and womanist nationalisms, gender difference works towards the same end for both: a means of imagining pure oppositionality.
Ultimately, it is this shared imaginative project that Stewart's *Productions*
put at risk by merging the languages of life and death.

4 ❧ BIO-POLITICAL RESISTANCE:

HARRIET BEECHER STOWE

Commitment to abolitionism links Stewart's speeches to the next text of domesticity I will read. But, despite the connections, social housekeeping in *Uncle Tom's Cabin* speaks in a strikingly different idiom—one reflecting intensifying educational and medical concern with the health and welfare of middle-class women and girls. This chapter presents domesticity in *Uncle Tom's Cabin* as resistance to a patriarchal educational system designed to prepare young women for the marriage market. Out of a critique addressing middle-class women's oppression, I argue, Stowe assembled the materials of her abolitionism.

Neither of Stowe's contestatory agendas detracts from the importance of critically scrutinizing her representation of African Americans or the race hierarchies Anglo-American abolitionism retained in its own rendering of emancipation.[1] Yet, *Uncle Tom's Cabin* serves this book's larger argument precisely because it forces us to confront the proximity between hegemony and resistance. Stowe's novel reduces the complex array of antebellum social relations into a single, apocalyptic contest between a patriarchal power which destroys selfhood and a womanist resistance which reinstates it. By transforming her critique of patriarchy into an analysis of slavery, Stowe identifies the situation of slaves with that of middle-class white women, and in doing so she obliterates the power differentials making their experiences incommensurable.[2] Stowe's act of identification depends upon domesticity's construction of gender difference. Women's nonparticipation in institutional politics guaranteed their fitness for the work of abolition because it demonstrated their allegedly apolitical status. Women's "powerlessness" circumvented inquiry into the hierarchies in which their expanded social

authority involved them, the activities they conducted not through institutionalized government but instead through informal, irregular, and
unofficial avenues—including cultural expression.

Yet, if *Uncle Tom's Cabin* lacks the political innocence which it claims
for itself, how can we talk about the novel without substantiating
Cooper's vision of a tyrannical mass culture controlled by women? How
can we acknowledge Stowe's involvement in antebellum power relations
and at the same time unsettle traditional critical assumptions about
popular women writers' dedication to preserving the status quo and
their prostration before ideology?

Reading Stowe without the gender binarisms through which the
canon has been constructed requires revising critical accounts of oppositionality. This chapter undertakes that assignment by locating the languages of patriarchal critique and abolition in *Uncle Tom's Cabin* within
the history of bio-politics and contemporary theory's attempts to de-
essentialize our conceptions of power and resistance.

Sentimental Hygiene

Throughout the decade before she wrote *Uncle Tom's Cabin,* Harriet
Beecher Stowe suffered from hysterical episodes that left her bedridden
for weeks at a time. These attacks were so severe that from May 1846 to
March 1847, she left her husband and their three young children in
Cincinnati for Dr. Wesselheoft's Hydropathic Institute, a fashionable
water-cure establishment in Brattleboro, Vermont, recommended to
her by her sister Catharine Beecher.[3]

The illness from which Stowe suffered in the 1840s may have, in part,
dictated her choice of subject matter for her abolitionist best-seller.
When read together, *Uncle Tom's Cabin* and Stowe's letters on her illness
suggest that the novelist identified the white hysterical housewife with
the black Southern slave, seeing both as victims of a patriarchal power
that violates the integrity of the self. Because the discourse on hysteria
addresses the issue of subjectivity at the same time that it expresses
concern for the health of the body, Stowe's figuration of the hysteric as
the archetypal victim of patriarchal government in *Uncle Tom's Cabin*
encodes (as I will explain in the next section of this chapter) both a
womanist and an abolitionist critique within hygienist norms. Stowe's
medicalizing of her attack on patriarchal government derives from her

sister Catharine Beecher's use of the concept of bodily economy in her writings on housekeeping and women's education. *Uncle Tom's Cabin* uses these materials to support abolitionist agitation that Beecher denounced.[4]

The biographical factors informing Stowe's political consciousness take shape within, and themselves evince, a larger restructuring of political power in relation to medical knowledge in the antebellum United States. Foucault suggests that "bio-power" or "bio-politics" (the integration of the medical and political) increasingly characterizes the exercise of governmental power in Western countries beginning in the eighteenth century.[5] Since that time "political technologies that [invest] the body, health, modes of subsistence and lodging" have proliferated—technologies directed toward "*policing*" but of a sort not to be "understood in the limiting, repressive sense we give the term today, but according to a much broader meaning that encompasse[s] all the methods for developing the quality of the population and the strength" of nations.[6] Reading the relation between Stowe's hysteria and political critique in *Uncle Tom's Cabin* articulates the history of the bio-political both as discourse and as "the materiality of power operating on the very bodies of individuals," in this case the body of the hysterical Stowe.[7]

Feminist scholarship has long recognized the status of both domestic ideology and *Uncle Tom's Cabin* as political critique, but my claim that such critique itself forms an important part of the history of the exercise of power might, at first, seem to imperil these readings. Jane Tompkins, for example, asserts that Stowe's novel delineates a feminist "*alterna-tive* . . . world, one which calls into question the whole structure of American society." In Tompkins's remark resistance stands in a relation-ship of alterity to political power and social institutions because it origi-nates *outside* of them and in the home. In the critical tradition repre-sented by Tompkins, only from such a privileged point can cultural critique transcend "the whole structure of . . . society."[8]

Although placing *Uncle Tom's Cabin* within the history of bio-power in the United States undermines oppositional analysis, it does *not* illustrate the containment of political resistance by that which it opposes. Bio-power renders irrelevant the power / resistance binarism upon which Tompkins's analysis depends. In *The History of Sexuality* Foucault replaces the binary with the multiple, asserting that society is "not a structure" but rather a network of "nonegalitarian and mobile" power relations. All of these relations have their limits. While he allows for "hegemonic effect" when some superstructural force "traverses the local opposi- tions" within otherwise competing power relations and "links them together," Foucault de-essentializes hegemony. A "whole" society to whose monolithic sameness resistance could oppose an equally mono- lithic difference does not exist; for Foucault, resistance to power cannot be grounded in radical alterity. Without a "binary and all-encompassing opposition between rulers and ruled at the root of power relations," there can be "no single locus of great Refusal, no soul of revolt, source of rebellions, or pure law of the revolutionary."[9] "Bio-political re- sistance" is not oxymoronic. Resistance must be retheorized as histor- ical rather than radical alterity. Against both Stowe's understanding of her own novel and first-wave feminist treatments of it, my reading of Stowe's bio-political critique of the patriarchal family and the institution of slavery analyzes political resistance as *defined* rather than *contained* by its entanglement in power relations.

Nervous White Women

A conflict between two perceptual modes, absorption and abstraction, structures Stowe's private letters on housekeeping from the late 1830s and the 1840s, and this conflict communicates the impact of the hygien- ist component of domestic ideology upon Stowe's interpretation of her own hysteria. These letters suggest that Stowe believed that she had a tendency to become absorbed in the physical details of domestic work and that, in order to recover from her illness, she needed to develop a household system, a domestic economy, to abstract herself from "minutiae."

In an 1845 letter to her husband, Stowe describes the drudgery of housework as a perilous visual activity. She describes herself not just (like all other nineteenth-century housewives) "working hard," but also "looking into closets, and seeing a great deal of that dark side of domes- tic life which a housekeeper may who will investigate too curiously into minutiae." If this letter represents the dark side of domestic labor as the somatic activity of focusing on particular household details, the specific symptomology of Stowe's hysteria represented a retreat from such ab- sorptive domestic vision. The author found herself paying for periods of intense domestic labor with ensuing episodes of hysterical blindness and a related "neuralgic complaint that settled in [her] eyes," which, as she put it, rendered her unable "to fix them with attention on anything."[10] Stowe was not so blinded by her hysteria as rendered unable to discern discrete objects. Confined to a darkened room during these attacks, she symbolically eluded absorptive vision at the same time that she actually eluded domestic labor.

Stowe's letters suggest that she imagined that her failure to impose a larger intellectual system or economy upon household specifics had resulted in her absorption in domestic details and her consequent illness. Stowe opposes absorption in domestic minutiae to what she calls "systematic" housekeeping. She writes to a friend in 1838 that "all [her] days [are] made up" of domestic "details," and in a later letter to her husband admits that she is "constitutionally careless and too impetuous and impulsive easily to maintain that consistency and order which is necessary in a family." The topic of "system and order in a family" inspires Stowe to effuse in one letter she wrote while at Brattleboro, "I know that nothing can be done without it; it is the keystone, the *sine qua non*. . . ." Systematic household organization, symbolizing the housewife's control over otherwise unorganized physical details, represents Stowe's attempt to imagine household labor as something more than manual labor. Expressing a rejection of absorptive domestic vision, Stowe's hysterical blindness answers her fear of being reduced to "but a mere drudge with few ideas."[11]

Like Stowe, Catharine Beecher understood hysteria as the result of absorption in details. In *Letters to the People on Health and Happiness* (1837), Beecher translates external multiplicity, the myriad of household details, into internal fragmentation, hysteria. Referring to the use of domestic help in wealthy families, Beecher laments the fact that even in the United States, where there is no genuine aristocracy, "one portion of the women have all the exercise of the *nerves of motion*, and another have all the *brain-work*." She explains the great virtue of properly systematic housework: "it would exercise every muscle in the body, and at the same time interest and exercise the mind." Disproportional development leads to self-division, hence the alarming incidence of "nervousness" and hysteria, for, when "equalization of the nervous fluid" is "withheld, the sensibility of the other portions of the brain is liable to become excessive, unnatural, and less under the control of the will."[12]

Beecher rapturously hails systematization as a way to make labor active rather than reactive, its stimulus being internal not external, determined by the housekeeper rather than by factors out of her control. Systematic housekeepers, she writes, "control circumstances" rather than allowing "circumstances control them."[13] Systematization prevents the self-division that causes "nervousness" among women.

The competing terms (discrete details versus overarching systems) shaping Stowe's interpretation of the origin of her illness also structure Beecher's domesticity. A single hygienist dictum informs virtually all of Beecher's writing on housekeeping: No faculty should be developed at the expense of any other. Disproportion must be avoided at all costs. Hysteria is the mark of patriarchal oppression. Beecher uses the concept of bodily economy to articulate a critique of patriarchal government of the home.[14] She, like other domestic ideologues committed to educational reform in the late eighteenth and early nineteenth centuries, believed that patriarchal interests had dictated the content of traditional female education.[15] In instructing girls exclusively in the ornamental graces requisite for obtaining an advantageous familial alliance through the marriage contract, that education had privileged the development of certain pleasing and marketable skills in women, accomplishments such as dancing and piano playing. Educational reformers lamented the rarified and partial product of such an upbringing. They responded with an educational method that they believed would cultivate the whole woman instead of only a few marketable accomplishments—hence Beecher's obsession with expelling any form of partiality from female experience.

Beecher tries to banish disproportion by organizing precisely those absorbing household details that her sister found so troublesome. "There is no one thing, more necessary to a housekeeper, in performing her varied duties," proclaims Beecher, who dedicates an entire chapter of her *Treatise on Domestic Economy* (1841) to the subject, "than *a habit of system and order,*" for "the affairs of a housekeeper [are] made up . . . of ten thousand desultory and minute items." In regard to the organization of the troublesome "minutiae of domestic arrangements," Beecher recommends that the housewife devote specific days to specific tasks. In a systematic household, Monday might be devoted to mending, Tuesday to washing, Wednesday to ironing, and so forth. For Beecher, the real issue is hygienic rather than merely practical, for a "wise economy is nowhere more conspicuous, than in the right *apportionment of time* to different pursuits." Systematization "modif[ies] any mistaken proportions" in a woman's development.[16] It allows her to cultivate various faculties instead of only a few.

Beecher links disproportion to the opening of a gap between mind and body. She designs her postpatriarchal pedagogy to heal this gap through the harmonious development of all the faculties (an economy of the body). For Beecher, domestic economy maintains bodily economy by encouraging women to exercise their will over physical details. In narrowing the gap between mind and body, domestic economy enhances subjectivity and thus combats hysteria.

Stowe's representation of absorptive labor, in an essay she wrote on nervousness, helps explain the logic of Beecher's belief that the housewife's enslavement to circumstances creates hysterical women. In "Irritability" the novelist speaks of overwork as an "overdraft on the nervous energy, which helps us to use up in one hour the strength of whole days" and compares it to alcohol, tobacco, and coffee (indulgences Beecher repeatedly denounces). According to Stowe, such stimulants permit one to shine "for a few hours of extra brightness," but with an artificial glow.[17] Artificial brightness, produced under the stimulus of excessive labor or narcotic indulgence, destabilizes subjectivity. To be stimulated artificially is to surrender self-determination and willpower and to make the body work independently of the mind. Beecher believes that systematization enhances female subjectivity by coordinating hand work and brain work, relocating the stimulus for activity within the housewife by creating an economy of the self in which all the faculties surrender control to the will.

Beecher's call for the educational conjunction of physical and intellectual culture partakes in a larger cultural grounding of female subjectivity in resistance to patriarchal control over the home. Other domestic ideologues (both British and U.S.) called for the creation of an integrated female self. These educators also wanted to institute the home, rather than the marriage market, as the focus of female education. If women were to spend the greater part of their adult lives in the home, then their education should prepare them for that life, not for a lifetime in the ballroom, the theater, or the drawing room. Hence Hannah More, the British author who influenced Beecher, asks, "Do we not educate [our daughters] for a crowd, forgetting they are to live at home? for the world, and not for themselves? for show, and not for use?"[18] According to More, patriarchal education engenders a craving for excitement that domestic life could never gratify and hence produced fragmented female selves, torn between desire and domestic duty. Domestic education of the sort envisaged first by More and later by Beecher represents the attempt to make duty and desire coincident, to imagine a form of household government that would enhance, not undermine, subjectivity.

Manualizers and Mentalizers

Because the sphere of female activity defined by Beecher and other female educators is circumscribed by the boundaries of the home, one could argue that domesticity was the extension rather than the subversion of patriarchal power. Carroll Smith-Rosenberg presents the hysterical woman as a rebel against the coercive ethos of "will, control, and hard work" personified in the ideal domestic woman, whom Smith-Rosenberg sees as the discursive product of patriarchal power.[19] As Jacques Donzelot points out, however, analyses such as these essentialize patriarchal hegemony. "For feminists," writes Donzelot, the rise of the domestic woman "seems of slight importance when weighed against a patriarchal domination seen as essentially unchanged across the centuries." The power / resistance binarism supporting Smith-Rosenberg's argument may "nurture . . . combat," but it also "conceals" historical changes in the family. Women's colleges, the growth of teaching and nursing as careers for women, the entrance of women into public life through their alliance with social professions—these were "the springboard" that women "needed for the recognition of [their] political rights."[20]

Even if such developments enforced behavioral norms and values that, to use Smith-Rosenberg's words, prepare women "to undertake the arduous and necessary duties of wife and mother,"[21] they also legitimated certain versions of female financial and social autonomy, without which female political enfranchisement was unthinkable. Although antebellum domesticity may at points intersect and even collaborate with patriarchal power, that fact does not make the former reducible to the latter. Nancy Armstrong has argued that British domestic ideology signals a "cultural change from an earlier form of power based on sumptuary display to a modern form that works through the production of subjectivity."[22] Armstrong's comment applies also to U.S. domesticity, which produces a female subject in the act of resisting patriarchal power.

Beecher's domestic ideology also bears resemblance to a late-eighteenth-century European educational analysis of the body's relationship to the state that, according to Donzelot, expressed itself through both a political discourse on the health and welfare of the working classes and a domestic discourse on the preservation of women and children. French educators, physicians, and politicians expressed a concern for the waste of labor resources through state oppression of the working classes at the same time that they exposed the "wasteful" and "artificial" education of the children of the wealthy. Valuable human resources were being squandered both at the bottom and the top of the social scale. The "impoverishment of the nation and the etiolation of its elite" would result, warned these authorities. Donzelot describes bio-politics as a two-part agenda, one emanating in a call for bodily economy to preserve the bodies of upper-class women and children and the other emanating in a call for social economy to preserve the bodies of the working classes.[23] Bio-political resistance unites the working classes with upper-class women and children against the patriarch. It demands that these two groups wrest control over their bodies away from him, stabilize their unstable subjectivities, and practice self-government.

Donzelot's account of bio-politics helps explain Stowe's apparent translation of the terms by which she understood her hysteria into a fictional representation of Southern slavery. In *Uncle Tom's Cabin* bodily economy and social economy merge in an abolitionist critique of patriarchal power. The very same hygienist logic undergirding Stowe's understanding of her hysteria governs Stowe's analysis of slavery, a coincidence suggested by the parallels her novel articulates between "nervous" white women and overworked black slaves.[24]

In *Uncle Tom's Cabin* the lack of an economy of the body among white women raised in unsystematic aristocratic households recapitulates in its structure the dissociation of mind and body produced by a society in which "a lower class" is "given up to physical toil and confined to an animal nature" so that "a higher one thereby acquires leisure and wealth for a more expanded intelligence and improvement, and becomes the directing soul of the lower."[25] This system, as proslavery apologist Henry Hughes put it, makes blacks "manualizers" and whites "mentalizers."[26]

The Southern white woman's lack of wholeness reflects and is predicated upon the division of labor into mentalizers and manualizers. Significantly, the hysterical and sickly Marie St. Clare is, as Stowe puts it, not a "whole woman." Rather she is, as Stowe twice repeats, "a fine figure, a pair of bright dark eyes, and a hundred thousand dollars" (1: 222, 224). The partial product of patriarchal education, the daughter raised for what Armstrong calls "sumptuary display," becomes an "unsystematic" housekeeper (1: 295). As in Beecher's narrative of the etiology of nervous disease, ill health in *Uncle Tom's Cabin* originates in the division between mind and body, a gap to whose presence Marie St. Clare's "enervated" nervous system (2: 144), her lapses into "hysterical spasms" (2: 118), and her failure to be a "whole woman" attest.

Even more vividly than Marie's hysterical outbursts, however, Little Eva's fatal illness suggests the bio-political dimension of Stowe's womanism. In representing Eva's slow decline, Stowe wages a bio-political critique of patriarchal power. The novelist describes Little Eva's body as something that is being used up too quickly. In her illness Eva, who is about eight years old, seems suddenly to undergo puberty. The consumptive flush, as has often been remarked of nineteenth-century representations of the disease, resembles the flush of awakening sexuality—a similarity that suggests that Stowe thinks of Eva, as much as the slave, as a victim of pre-industrial Southern discipline. Eva's father Augustine St. Clare notes something unnatural and precocious about his daughter. He is struck by "the daily increasing maturity of the child's mind and feelings," and all notice a new "womanly thoughtfulness" gracing Eva's behavior as her disease progresses (2: 67).

Contemporaneous discussions of consumption further substantiate my claim that Eva's illness functions as a symbol for the dissociation of mind and body produced by patriarchal government. Dr. William Alcott advises that the "common custom of pushing forward the intellect at the expense of the body" lies behind many cases of consumption.[27] Alcott sees in consumption a failure to maintain an economy of the body, a dangerous and disproportionate development of one faculty (the imagination) at the expense of development of another faculty (the body).

Moreover, in the dissociation of mind and body depicted in Eva's illness, the novelist creates a version of her own hysteria. At one point St. Clare wonders if Eva isn't growing "nervous"—a suggestion that Eva dismisses, although the narrator notes "a nervous twitching about the corners of her [Eva's] mouth" (2: 28). As Dr. James Clark, a midcentury authority on consumption, writes, there "is more nervous sensibility than is natural to the [consumptive] patient," and Alcott concurs.[28] According to Stowe, the nervous are "soon used up" or consumed.[29] Little Eva's precociousness, the rapid consumption of her flesh, her apparent nervous susceptibility, all express Stowe's critique of a patriarchal power that discourages proportional development in women and deprives them of self-government.[30]

In *Uncle Tom's Cabin* the South uses up black slaves even more conspicuously than it consumes white women. Stowe deems slave labor in the southernmost states of the Union less hygienic than those of more northerly regions, for the "general prevalence of agricultural pursuits of a quiet and gradual nature, not requiring those periodic seasons of hurry and pressure that are called for in the business of more southern districts, makes the task of the negro [in states like Kentucky] a more healthful and reasonable one" (1: 23). Because preindustrial Southern labor is task- rather than time-oriented, Stowe can transform the intense physical activity of slaves engaged in absorptive labor into a kind of consumptive fever. As Simon Legree summarizes his treatment of slaves, "Use up, and buy more, 's my way . . ." (2: 173). During the "heat and hurry of the [cotton-picking] season" (2: 183), the overseer's whip temporarily "stimulate[s]" slaves "to an unnatural strength" (2: 191), and hence, in the logic of mid-century hygiene, the bodies of blacks are used up all the more quickly. The term "used up" adumbrates the hygienist maxim upon which "Irritability" dilates: it is better to "labor for years steadily, diligently . . . avoiding those cheating stimulants that overtax Nature" than "to pass life in exaltations and depressions, resulting from overstrained labors, supported by unnatural stimulus."[31] The patriarchal stimulus to labor is unnatural in that it comes from outside rather than from within and hence leaves the slave exhausted.

There is nothing remarkable about the fact that Stowe's representation of Southern slavery should refer to the horrific intensity of slave labor in the fields. Obviously, attention to the physical effects of slavery on the body furthers both Stowe's realism and her polemic intent; however, that Stowe embeds her critique of coercive power in the specific logic of bodily economy *does* warrant remark.

Hygienist notions of absorptive labor, and their implicit womanist critique, even determine Stowe's representation of slave labor of a less intensive variety than fieldwork. The St. Clare's cook Dinah reproduces the Southern disciplinary system in her method of managing the St. Clare kitchen. Stowe notes that, even though the kitchen is generally characterized by disorder of the most extreme variety, Dinah "had, at irregular periods, paroxysms of reformation and arrangement, which she called 'clarin' up times'" (1: 302). Labor manifests itself like a spasm or a fever in these "irregular periods." Stowe's language suggests an analogy between Dinah's "clarin' up times" and those "periodic seasons of heat and hurry" characteristic of fieldwork when she refers to the cook's occasional attempts to put the kitchen in order as "periodic seasons" of household reform (1: 302).

Dinah's spasmodic relation to labor symbolizes her spasmodic relation to discipline, the gap patriarchal government generates between power and the subject, the same gap that Stowe suggests in her representation of Marie St. Clare's lack of "wholeness" and of Little Eva's illness. Stowe's hygienist critique of patriarchal government stresses the inadequacy of disciplinary technologies that disrupt the economy of the self. My point is not that Stowe addresses issues of the body but rather that a nineteenth-century concept of physical health structures the entire logic of Stowe's critique of patriarchal power. Stowe's critique, in other words, is bio-political.

Mind / Body Binarisms

The integration of the political and the medical increasingly characterizes U.S. society in the antebellum period, and both Beecher's domesticity and Stowe's abolitionism evince this integration in their encoding of political critique within a hygienist logic. Both authors configure the violation of the integrity of the subject effected by patriarchal power as a disruption of the integrity of the animal economy, as a gap created between manual and mental, as hysteria.

While Stowe translated her belief in the need for an economy of the body into an abolitionist best-seller, Beecher's hygienist fear of the partial and the detail led her to oppose abolitionism. In her *Essay on Slavery and Abolitionism* (1837), Beecher represents the antislavery movement as a variety of mania by which "the minds of men are thrown into a ferment." Abolitionist leaders, writes Beecher, are probably otherwise moral and reasonable individuals, but because of political measures that require disproportionate fixation on a single idea, a significant portion of

the movement's leadership is composed of "men accustomed to a contracted field of observation, and more qualified to judge of immediate
results than of general tendencies."[32] Bio-power determines the discursive materials through which various political positions articulate themselves but does not completely determine individual interpretations of
those materials into specific political affiliations.

Because the materials of bio-power are subject to multiple, although
not infinite, interpretations and uses, Foucault asks that we reconceive
power as "power relations" and resistance as "resistances";[33] however,
in the particular versions of bio-politics represented in Beecher's and
Stowe's work, the integration of the political and the medical discourages us from thinking of the relationship between power and resistance as anything other than a "binary and all-encompassing opposition." Perhaps we should think of bio-politics not as a particular political
interest or stance so much as a way of conceiving the political. Beecher's
hygienist analysis of abolitionism is really less concerned with that particular movement than it is with a condemnation of politics in general.
Any engagement in politics, for Beecher, threatens the self (throws "the
mind of men . . . into a ferment"), because all political beliefs are partial
and involve devotion to details at the expense of larger systems. Any
relation to power, whether as its victim (in the case of the hysterical
housewife) or as its agent (in the case of the hysterical abolitionist), leads
to self-division.

To imagine power as something that creates self-division is to imagine
power as simultaneously absolute and negative. In discussing the "separation in the subject between *psyche* and *soma*" figured in hysteria, D. A.
Miller suggests that, paradoxically, the hysteric, whom Stowe likens to
the slave, may be the figure of the liberal subject par excellence. Hysteria, Miller writes, allows us to imagine the radical autonomy of the individual from the society around her, for "what the body suffers, the
mind needn't think."[34] The body of the hysteric, like the body of the
slave, is coerced by power, but the mind of both hysteric and slave
remains absent and aloof. In Stowe's and Beecher's bio-political imaginations, the nervous woman and the slave are archetypal objects of power,
but the hygienist body / mind binarism built into the representation of
hysteric and slave does not permit them to become the subjects of
power. Subjectivity, selfhood, and individualism are invested in one half
of the binarism whereas political relations, power, and society pertain

only to the other half. This negative inscription of power enables the oppositionalist understanding of resistance. The hysteric and the slave, as discursive entities, serve simultaneously as figures of utter disempowerment and transcendental resistance, of a resistance whose purity is guaranteed by its radical alterity from what Tompkins calls "the whole structure of society."

That the mind and body could become utterly dissevered, no matter how oppressive the circumstances, is, at best, a dubious proposition. If people could be made into mere bodies, slavery would seem less appalling than it does. Henry Hughes's division of society into manualizers and mentalizers rests on a proposition not just offensive but nonsensical: that some people are things. Stowe's original subtitle for her novel—*The Man That Was a Thing*—conveys the absurdity of the legal fiction that makes subjects into objects. It expresses the pathos of the situation of human beings treated as though they were simply bodies, and yet, paradoxically, Stowe's concept of resistance to enslavement requires that sometimes people be things.

Even when Stowe represents the resistance to patriarchal government that her novel would appear to legitimate, the hygienist mind / body binarism allows her to imagine the self in a relation of complete exteriority to the political power exercised in the act of rebellion. When George Harris can no longer tolerate his master's abuse and determines to escape slavery or die trying, Stowe represents this as George's loss of control over his body. He "had [formerly] been able to repress every disrespectful word; but the flashing eye, the gloomy and troubled brow, were part of a natural language that could not be repressed,—indubitable signs, which showed too plainly that the man could not become a thing" (1: 29). Curiously, in the very moment that George becomes determined to be more than a body, more than a thing, Stowe reduces him to his body.

When George's wife Eliza learns her master has sold their son to a slave trader, she too loses the capacity for self-government. Although she believes she is "wicked" to run away, she explains to her friends that she "can't help it" (1: 63, 64). One expresses approbation of her actions by asserting that Eliza did "what no kind o' mother could help a doin'!" (1: 139). Eliza's loss of control over her body manifests itself in "pale, shivering . . . rigid features and compressed lips" that make her look like "an entirely altered being from the soft and timid creature she had been hitherto" (1: 60). Not until she has reached Indiana with her son does the "supernatural tension of [her] nervous system [lessen]" and the apparently hysterical Eliza fall into a sort of nervous exhaustion (1: 82).

Stowe's insistence on the mind/body binarism in her representation of first George's and then Eliza's acts of resistance allows the body to suffer "what the mind needn't think." These two episodes record Stowe's inability to conceive of the subject in any relation to the political. Rebellion in *Uncle Tom's Cabin* is not a political act but rather the radical separation of the individual from all political activity. In Stowe's mind, power and resistance are so polarized that she cannot imagine resistance as the assertion of a legitimate political position against an illegitimate one. Instead the novelist represents resistance as what Foucault calls the "great soul of revolt," a radically independent self, rebelling against political power in general, rather than some particular and malignant manifestation of power.

Stowe's inability to think of the subject in relation to the political is perhaps even clearer in her characterization of the abolitionist Ophelia's demeanor. St. Clare's cousin from Vermont is as "inevitable as a clock, and as inexorable as a railroad engine." The mechanical metaphors express her disdain for "all modes of procedure which [have] not a direct and inevitable relation to accomplishment of some purpose then definitely had in mind" (1: 229). Stowe represents Ophelia (in what has to be a significant metaphor in an abolitionist novel) as the "absolute bond-slave" of her personal moral code (1: 230), including her abolitionism. Despite Ophelia's obedience to a political creed rather than external coercion, Stowe suggests with Ophelia's machine-like deportment a self-division comparable to that of the slave laboring under the whip. Although St. Clare's cousin comes from an abolitionist family and expresses strong political views on the issue of slavery, Stowe undermines the legitimating grounds of abolitionism as a political position when she shows Ophelia recoiling in horror at the sight of whites touching black slaves. Ophelia's automatonism suggests that the gap between the subject and the political cannot be bridged.

Even though Simon Legree represents a political position antithetically opposed to Ophelia's, Stowe understands his proslavery ideology too as fundamentally exterior to the self. The novel's final chapters, which show Legree descending into alcoholism and insanity, suggest that Stowe's villain had all along been maddeningly ambivalent about the morality of slavery and that only a Herculean act of self-government, analogous to Ophelia's enslavement to her politics, enabled him to hold slaves in the first place. Significantly, when Legree's self-control begins to unravel, Stowe symbolizes it with an image of the body uncannily coming to life. On her deathbed Eva gives a lock of her hair to Tom, who later comes into Legree's possession. This lock of hair "like a living thing, twine[s] itself round Legree's fingers" and his memories when he confiscates it from Tom (2: 216). Eva's memento animates Legree's long dead memory of another lock of hair that also "twined about his fingers" (2: 218)—this one a token from his saintly mother's deathbed. Legree wonders "if hair could rise from the dead!" (2: 220). What has actually risen from the dead are Legree's repressed feelings, the self buried safely out of reach from politics. The uncanny quality of this scene consists in the body's (the hair's) refusal to act like a *thing*. Stowe configures Legree's eroding ability to repress those emotions as the body uncannily taking on a life of its own.[35]

Integrating the medical and the political permits Stowe to imagine in the split between body and mind a transcendent liberal subject radically independent of political power and society in general. One episode especially conveys how absorptive vision returns as the novelist's abolitionist desideratum. Augustine St. Clare compares the danger of looking too minutely into the details of the slave system to the danger of looking too closely into his cook Dinah's slovenly habits of kitchen management. "If we are to be prying and spying into all the dismals of life," he informs his Northern cousin Miss Ophelia, who asks him how he can live with his knowledge of the abuse suffered by slaves, "we should have no heart to anything. 'T is like looking too close into the details of Dinah's kitchen . . ." (2: 8). St. Clare later quotes the axiom by which his father conveniently disposed of the matter of the maltreatment of slaves: "General rules will bear hard on particular cases" (2: 17).

In her letters on hysteria Stowe represents herself as a "housekeeper" who "investigate[s] too curiously into minutiae." Stowe was committed to eliciting on behalf of her political cause the absorptive vision and commitment to the particular that St. Clare disavows. According to *A Key to Uncle Tom's Cabin* (1853), general rules, like those promoted by St. Clare, have impeded emancipation: "The atrocious and sacrilegious system," Stowe claims, referring to the institution of slavery, "fails to produce the impression on the mind that it ought to produce because it is lost in generalities." She concludes that she herself "cannot give any idea of the horribly cruel and demoralizing effect of [slavery], except by presenting facts in detail."[36] Facts in detail, investigation into minutiae, absorptive vision—these can topple political belief and abstract theories. Whereas Stowe's earlier letters on hysteria express a Beecherian denunciation of detail in favor of system, in *Uncle Tom's Cabin* the hysterical violation of economy and wholeness entailed by privileging detail functions simultaneously as the product of patriarchal power and the grounds of resistance to it.

Resistance and Alterity

Clearly *Uncle Tom's Cabin* does not fulfill its own fantasy of itself as radically liberatory across a range of race and class hierarchies, but that does not deprive it of all oppositional force. The novel helped legitimate two historically momentous and politically progressive platforms: abolition and white middle-class women's intervention in putatively "masculine" concerns. Domesticity, however, accomplishes these feats by producing female and African American subjects in opposition to its figures of the patriarch / slaveholder. Forums advocating household and social reform in the name of health and welfare made this subjectivity normative. The assertion that domesticity produced subjects, with desires and not simply duties, may seem to make its power utterly determinative—but only because we (like Stowe) have no way to articulate agency except through evidence of the self's radical autonomy.

The difficulty of divesting our political imaginations of the prophylactic binarism, the difficulty of imagining a *subject* of power, is suggested by the tendency of even Foucauldian literary criticism to depend upon a body / mind dyad in describing how power works. Foucauldian critics speak of power in the nineteenth century as "internalized . . . institutional control" and the "inward" relocation of "external discipline's traditional corrective tools."[37] To understand bio-power as internalized physical discipline, as the introjection of the prison cell or the slave master's whip, is to apply the mind / body binarism to consciousness itself. In these tropes power stands in a belated relation to subjectivity. Foucault interrogates this strictly negative concept of power when he questions the "repressive hypothesis" in *The History of Sexuality*. In figuring power as introjected social control, these critics fail to challenge "a human subject on the lines of the model provided by classical philosophy, endowed with a consciousness which power is then thought to seize on."[38] In *Discipline and Punish* Foucault insists that we "must cease once and for all to describe the effects of power in negative terms." Power "produces," he writes, and precisely what it produces is a subject.[39]

Foucauldian criticism on nineteenth-century literature has also tended to define resistance as radical alterity—no doubt because of the difficulty of imagining a productive relationship between the self and power. Inspired by *The History of Sexuality*'s assertion that where "there is power, there is resistance, and yet, or rather consequently, this resistance is never in a position of exteriority in relation to power," it has deconstructed the central binarism of oppositional criticism by demonstrating how political critique fails to occupy such a position of exteriority and hence is recuperated by power. Only within the logic of the oppositionalist binarism, however, are the failure to stand outside of power and the recuperation of resistance synonymous. Resistance may not transcend power relations altogether, but that does not mean that it merely reproduces the same power relations or that all power relations must reproduce the status quo.

Nor does thinking of bio-power as having a productive relation to the self render the subject a mere pawn of social control. Foucault writes that bio-power's

> subject constitutes himself in an active fashion, by the practices of self, these practices are nevertheless not something that the individual invents by himself. They are patterns that he finds in his culture and which are proposed, suggested and imposed on him by his culture, his society and his social group.[40]

Judith Butler suggests an alternative model of subjectivity in relation to power which does not depend upon the existence of the liberal subject radically free of "the whole structure of society." Butler describes a "cultural self" created as a "process of interpretation within a network of deeply entrenched cultural norms."[41] Power invests this "cultural self" in both positive and nondeterminist ways because it works not as a limit on thought but instead as the grounds for it.

As a mass phenomenon which traversed multiple fields of discourse, domesticity appears to be one of the most highly codified norms of the antebellum era. Even so, it required interpretation and enactment within these various fields. Reading *Uncle Tom's Cabin* and Stowe's letters on housekeeping in relationship to Beecher's domesticity usefully problematizes the determinism both Foucault and Butler question. Stowe's investment in her sister's household philosophy was so thorough as to constitute her experience of physical illness, but reinterpreted within the discourse of race, it helped Stowe formulate a position in direct conflict with Beecher's stance on abolition and authorized middle-class women's interventions into political controversies. Stowe obviously did not transcend her culture; she worked within the discourse of domesticity to articulate two monumentally important instances of opposition, instances of the historical alterity Foucault and Butler describe rather than the radical alterity that womanist politics ascribes to itself.

The subjectivity that domesticity generates grows out of resistance (to patriarchy)—hence its purveyors' sense of affinity with multiple sites of controversy, which they frequently misunderstand, misrepresent, and misuse; however, disseminated by middle-class women among other populations through the activities of social housekeeping, domestic womanhood still left itself open to different kinds of enactment. Hence the conclusion of a reading of domesticity should be not that resistance is futile but rather that its work is never done.

5 ❧ HOMOSOCIAL ROMANCE:

NATHANIEL HAWTHORNE

The very inmost soul of [Dimmesdale] seemed to be brought out before [Chillingworth's] eyes, so that he could see and comprehend its every movement. He became . . . not a spectator only, but a chief actor, in the poor minister's interior world. He could play upon him as he chose. —Nathaniel Hawthorne, *The Scarlet Letter*[1]

Critics have long associated the gothic with all that is considered "decadent," including homosexuality. More recently, Eve Kosofsky Sedgwick has specified the terms of this association by identifying a group of late-eighteenth- and early-nineteenth-century British gothic novels that share a paranoid plot. In them a male character "not only is persecuted by, but considers himself transparent to and often under the compulsion of, another male."[2]

Hawthorne's *The Scarlet Letter* describes precisely such an instance of one man's subjection to another male's gaze and will. The Dimmesdale-Chillingworth plot grows in part out of an 1839 notebook entry in which Hawthorne records his interest in the psychic state which we would now call "paranoia." The entry reads: "The strange sensation of a person who feels himself an object of deep interest, and close observation, and various construction of all his actions, by another person."[3] Under Chillingworth's reign of terror, Dimmesdale becomes so paranoid that he is unable to recognize his real enemy, even though that man has moved into his home. "Mr. Dimmesdale," explains the narrator, "would perhaps have seen this individual's character more perfectly, if a certain morbidness, to which sick hearts are liable, had not rendered him suspicious of all mankind. Trusting no man as his friend, he could not recognize his enemy . . ." (130).

In the psychodynamics of the erotic triangle underwriting the plot of Hawthorne's text, Hester Prynne (the feminine term) serves as little more than a pretext for an affective exchange between men. Robert Penn Warren remarked that "the two men are more important to each other than Hester is to either" and that "theirs is the truest marriage."[4] Sedgwick proposes (drawing from Rene Girard) that often "the bonds of 'rivalry' and 'love,' differently as they are experienced, are equally powerful and in many senses equivalent."[5] Hawthorne's narrator encourages a similar line of inquiry into the rivalry between his male characters, asking "whether hatred and love be not the same thing at bottom":

> Each, in its utmost development, supposes a high degree of intimacy and heart-knowledge; each renders one individual dependent for the food of his affections and spiritual life upon another; each leaves the passionate lover, or the no less passionate hater, forlorn and desolate by the withdrawal of his object. (260)

The Scarlet Letter provokes interpretation of "passion" in sexual terms. The narrator describes Chillingworth's assault on Dimmesdale as if it were rape: the doctor "probes," "burrows," "violates." Chillingworth's mysterious demise at the end of the story adheres to this sexual trajectory by conjuring up an image of detumescence. Having finally achieved the "completest triumph and consummation" of his plot against the minister, the physician's "strength and energy . . . seemed at once to desert him," and he "positively withered up" and "shriveled away" (260). One wonders, *pace* Ernest Sandeen, if *The Scarlet Letter* isn't a love story after all.[6]

The scarcity of commentary on *The Scarlet Letter*'s homoerotic subtext is striking, particularly in light of the wealth of criticism addressing sexual equivocality in the works of the other canonical writers of Hawthorne's time (Melville, Cooper, Whitman).[7] Perhaps the relative visibility of traditional heterosexual relations in Hawthorne's biography explains the reticence. Because of the publication of his love letters to his wife Sophia Peabody Hawthorne and his notebook entries recording the behavior and growth of his three children, Hawthorne's artistic genius has been cast in solidly heterosexual terms.[8] Henry James, for example, believed that Hawthorne "lived primarily in his domestic affections, which were of the tenderest kind."[9] A more contemporary critic pronounces Hawthorne "the most perfectly domestic of all [the male canonical] American writers, the one most devoted to the family as the scene of fulfilling relation."[10]

The argument of this chapter poses no threat to Hawthorne's staunchly heterosexual reputation. Nor will it attempt to relocate *The Scarlet Letter* in the expanding list of "classic American" gay crypto-texts. I begin with the question of the erotic ambiguity because ambiguity so often serves as a critical touchstone, marking the political and literary difference between the work of male mid-century canonical writers and their female contemporaries. This chapter will show that reading the ties between linguistic ambiguity and erotic ambiguity in Hawthorne's homosocial plot is the first step in removing the touchstone, which I argue is also a stumbling block for understanding the politics of women's domestic fiction.

Modernism and the "American Renaissance"

The Chillingworth-Dimmesdale plot does not bespeak its author's or its male characters' repressed or manifest sexuality so much as the structural conditions of male-male relationships in the homophobic culture which we share with Hawthorne.[11] Sedgwick describes an underlying but occasionally visible "continuum between homosocial and homosexual" exercising influence over these relationships. There exists, she writes, a "tendency toward important correspondences and similarities between the most sanctioned forms of male-homosocial bonding, and the most reprobated expressions of male homosexual sociality." This is because "paths of male entitlement in Euro-American societies [require] certain intense male bonds": "male friendship, mentorship, admiring identification, bureaucratic subordination, and heterosexual rivalry." The minimal articulation of difference between homosocial and homosexual fosters the instability characteristic of representations of male-male relationships:

> the fact that what goes on at football games, in fraternities, at the Bohemian Grove, and at climactic moments in war novels can look, with only a slight shift of optic, quite startlingly "homosexual," is not most importantly an expression of the psychic origin of these institutions in a repressed or sublimated homosexual genitality. In-

stead, it is the coming to visibility of the normally implicit terms of a coercive double bind. . . . For a man to be a man's man is separated only by an invisible, carefully blurred, always-already-crossed line from being "interested in men."

Sedgwick's double bind represents more than a paradox; it functions strategically, ensuring that homosocial paths of male entitlement simultaneously secure male hegemony and leave men (homosexual or otherwise) open to policing and self-policing through "the leverage of homophobia."[12] Even if it were possible, out-ing Hawthorne would merely satisfy the logic of minimal difference upon which our culture manufactures the all-important but ever-unstable difference between homosocial and homosexual.

Of course, critics have commented at length upon *The Scarlet Letter*'s perspectival shifts—but not typically in relation to the text's sexual and gender politics. In particular, the meteor scene in "The Minister's Vigil" has provoked a great deal of commentary. In that chapter, Dimmesdale mounts the scaffold where years earlier Hester had stood at mid-day. Making her way home from the governor's sickbed with Pearl, Hester happens upon Dimmesdale. After the family is reunited on the scaffold, a meteor illuminates the midnight sky. The meteor, writes Hawthorne,

> showed the familiar scene of the street, with the distinctness of mid-day, but also with the awfulness that is always imparted to familiar objects by an unaccustomed light. The wooden houses, with their jutting stories and quaint gable-peaks; the doorsteps and thresholds, with the early grass springing up about them; the garden-plots, black with freshly turned earth; the wheel-track, little worn, and, even in the market-place, margined with green on either side;—all were visible, but with a singularity of aspect that seemed to give another moral interpretation to the things of this world than they had ever borne before. (154)

Several critics have located the politics of Hawthorne's aesthetics in such shifts of optics. For example, Evan Carton proposes that "*The Scarlet Letter* and the meteor are subversive in the same subtle way: each produces an illumination that unsettles the objectivity of objects by revealing the act of perception that figures in their constitution." De-

scribing a position taken by other critics, Carton writes that, by exposing reality "as multiply and irresolvably interpreted," Hawthorne "chal-
lenges a fundamentalist understanding of perception, morality, and language [and] frustrates the attempt to validate them by reference to a
reality that exists prior to and independent of their operations."[13]

Moreover, critics have based claims for Hawthorne's modernism or
premodernism on his optic shifts and the self-reflexivity they are said to
indicate. In David Leverenz's view, Hawthorne and other American
Renaissance authors "help[ed] to inaugurate the modernist tradition of
alienated mind play" and threw one of the first punches in the "modernist sparring match between avant-garde writers and bourgeois readers."[14] Another critic asserts that "the theory of the Romance," developed in large part in response to Hawthorne's work, "allowed
America's nineteenth-century novelists to be seen as prototypes of
alienated modern artists."[15]

These critical statements suggest a way of reframing my initial reading of the Chillingworth-Dimmesdale plot within the critical param-
eters of modernist aesthetics; however, such a reframing neither contains nor diminishes the relevance of the sexual and gender protocols to
Hawthorne's optic shifts. After all, the canon of the premodernist
American Renaissance has been steadfastly homosocial. Furthermore,
as Nina Baym suggests, its homosociality is constitutional; it is impossible to insert women writers into a canon whose coherence depends
upon their serving as its other.[16] One cannot, for example, include
women writers in Leverenz's American Renaissance because he articulates self-reflexivity along the antimonies of gender (however histor-
icized) when he asserts that the "feminization" of the profession of
letters meant that male writers felt out of place in an occupation where
women writers could feel at home. "Male writers developed premodernist styles to explore and exalt their sense of being deviant from male
norms" while women writers felt no alienation and therefore clung to
the familiar realist style. "Unlike the women writers" of the antebellum
period, "classic male writers" satisfy the expectations of contemporary
critics by "[destabilizing] their narrations" and creating texts with "false
bottoms."[17]

Even a feminist-identified critic like Leverenz reconstructs the
American Renaissance along male homosocial lines because, as Leverenz's thesis indicates, definitions of literary modernism remain stead-

fastly homosocial, dependent upon a gendered schematics in which men
have an imagined special access to alienation and self-alienation.[18] Thus,
reframing Hawthorne's optic shifts within critical accounts of the modernism of the mid-century classic in no way disposes of sexuality and
gender as relevant analytic categories. To the contrary, as I will argue over the course of this chapter, contemporary critical understanding
of the self-reflexivity of Hawthorne's premodernist novel is entirely
obligated to the sex/gender system Hawthorne figures through his
perspectival shifts.[19]

Hawthorne's Homosocial Idyll

My conviction in the necessity of juxtaposing *The Scarlet Letter*'s erotic
ambiguities with the critical discussion of self-reflexive texts grows out
of interpretation of several of Hawthorne's early works representing
relationships between men. *The Scarlet Letter*'s perspectival disruptions
constitute one link in a chain of associations extending across Hawthorne's earlier fictional and nonfictional writing and wedding his premodernist aesthetics to male homosociality.

The chain begins in the summer of 1837 when Hawthorne took up
residence for five weeks in Augusta, Maine, at the home of Horatio
Bridge (a college chum who would become Hawthorne's lifelong patron
and, ultimately, his biographer).[20] Hawthorne's notebook entries from
this period depict a paradise of bachelors worthy of Melville himself.
According to *The American Notebooks,* Hawthorne, Bridge, and a French
boarder by the name of M. Schaeffer lived together at Bridge's house "in
great harmony and brotherhood" (46). Like other nineteenth-century
male homosocial idylls, Hawthorne's figures as an escape from the manners, mores, and morals of what Huck Finn would later call "sivilia-
tion." Comments Hawthorne in one entry from this period, "I think I
should soon become strongly attached to our way of life—so independent, and untroubled by the forms of restrictions of society" (34).[21]

In the notebook entries male homosocial relations are more than just
one thematic locale ripe for perspectival disruptions. The minimal difference between homosocial and homosexual (along with the heightened scrutiny and self-scrutiny minimal difference entails in an all-male
setting) guaranteed that relations among the three men would be particularly productive of perspectival shifts. Initially, Hawthorne found

M. Schaeffer slightly repulsive and dismissed him as "a queer little Frenchman" (32); however, over the course of his residence, Hawthorne came to admire Schaeffer's intelligence and to identify with his "queerness." One comment suggests that Hawthorne saw Schaeffer in a role that he would increasingly claim for himself, alien(ated) intellectual trying to make his living off a dullard bourgeoisie:

> The little Frenchman impresses me very strongly . . . so lonely as he is here, struggling against the world, with bitter feelings in his breast . . . enjoying here what little domestic comfort and confidence there is for him; and then going about all the live-long day, teaching French to blockheads who sneer at him. . . . (33)

Bridge's recollections make it clear that the bond that developed between the three men grew out of a shared sense of economic failure, for which lack of domestic comfort in the form of a wife and family became the sign.[22] Soon Hawthorne began referring to himself as "a queer character" (34). And before his stay at Bridge's bachelor establishment had ended, he wrote that all three of its residents were "as queer a set as may be found anywhere," living "as queer a life as any body leads" (46).

Of course, at the time "queer" did not have the sexual connotation that today may very well constitute its primary meaning. But contemporary usage is not entirely beside the point. Although Hawthorne never clarifies what it is exactly that makes him and his roommates so queer, in context the word seems to refer primarily to the trio's deviance from antebellum norms of male heterosexual subjectivity. All three men were bachelors, and (like Queequeg and Ishmael in bed at the beginning of *Moby Dick*) they composed what at the time could only be conceived of as a parody of proper heterosexual domesticity. Hawthorne was thirty-three years old, and his romantic experiences had (in the words of Edwin Haviland Miller) been limited to "voyeurism" and "fantasies."[23] According to *The American Notebooks*, Bridge had "almost . . . made up his mind never to be married" (33), and Schaeffer "had never yet sinned with woman" (46).

Augusta, then, was an atmosphere ripe for sexual equivocality. "Queer" records this equivocality, and it also suggests the connection in homophobic cultures between male homosociality and the sensation of perspectival shift. Hawthorne's feeling of liberation from social constraints ensued from his sense that he was (to borrow the language of

"The Minister's Vigil") seeing familiar things in an unaccustomed light. In his paradise of bachelors, the heightened vigilance elicited by Schaeffer (*"He's queer!"*) fomented parallel estrangements (*"I guess if I didn't know Bridge as well as I do, I'd think he was queer too . . ."*), culminating in the defamiliarization of what is most familiar, the self (*"Come to think of it, I guess I'm pretty queer myself!"*).

Consciously or unconsciously Hawthorne continued to associate such moments of self-reflection with homosocial interaction. What purports to be the translator's preface to his tale "Rappaccini's Daughter" (1844) perhaps best exemplifies the self-reflexive quality of Hawthorne's later imaginative writing. The preface is self-reflexive in the most literal sense. In it, Hawthorne scrutinizes himself, but does so as if he were another man—a stranger, an alien, one M. de l'Aubepine. In this supremely ironic assessment of his own literary reputation, Hawthorne, significantly, attributes his tale to the fictitious Aubepine, the "French-ification" of "Hawthorne" that the queer M. Schaeffer had affectionately bestowed upon him during his residence in Augusta.[24]

That detail, along with the fact that "Rappaccini's Daughter" records a quasi-gothic struggle of will between two men (Giovanni and Rappaccini), suggests a symbolic circuit in Hawthorne's mind between looking at other men and looking at himself. Hence the resemblance between the 1838 notebook entry describing intensive scrutiny of another man ("the strange sensation of a person who feels himself an object of deep interest, and close observation, and various construction of all his actions, by another person") and an entry made one year earlier describing intensive scrutiny of oneself as if one were another man:

> A perception, for a moment, of one's eventual and moral self, as if it were another person,—the observant faculty being separated, and looking intently at the qualities of the character. There is a surprise when this happens,—this getting out of oneself,—and then the observer sees how queer a fellow he is. (178)

The Scarlet Letter's Dimmesdale-Chillingworth plot brings the two notebook entries together by coupling the "homo-" with the "auto-". Chillingworth's ambiguous ontological status (Is he a gothic persecutor or a projection of Dimmesdale's troubled conscience?) supports Sedgwick's attempt to trace a literary historical genealogy connecting the paranoid gothic to high male modernism. The gothic novel's representation of "two potent male figures locked in an epistemologically indissoluble clench of will and desire," she insists, was evacuated of its sexual contents and refigured as the man at war with himself, the theme of modern man's divided consciousness.[25] Although *The Scarlet Letter* lends itself this psychological interpretation, it does not erase the sexual anxiety suffusing its homosocial plot; nor do Hawthorne's early notebook entries describing the sensation of looking at himself ever entirely disown their kinship to the experience of being looked at by another man—and being revealed as "a queer fellow" in the process.

Men Looking at Themselves

Historicizing Hawthorne's "revolutionary" aesthetics also requires attention to the structural presence women have by virtue of their absence from *The Scarlet Letter*'s homosocial plot. Robert K. Martin writes that Hawthorne's subversive aesthetics originate in estrangement and that "estrangement . . . was foreclosed to most American women of Hawthorne's time, who were increasingly bound to the familiar limitations of the domestic."[26] The next two sections of this chapter propose that critics have not been able to detach their estimations of Hawthorne's literary value from their figurations of a feminized realm of domestic familiarity because Hawthorne himself labored so hard to make them appear indissoluble.

Even after Hawthorne entered into a traditional heterosexual relationship by marrying Sophia Peabody, he persisted in thematizing his estrangement from the domestic in his correspondence and his notebooks. Not until shortly before his death would Hawthorne declare that he was, finally, "beginning to take root . . . and feel myself, for the first time in my life, really at home."[27] Despite frequent references to his domestic felicity, Hawthorne was strangely predisposed to see himself partaking in that joy from a distance. In a comment that links him to the voyeuristic Miles Coverdale in *The Blithedale Romance,* Hawthorne tells of the regret he feels when he retires to bed at night, leaving the parlor with its evidence of family life behind: "after closing the sitting-room door, I re-open it, again and again, to peep back at the warm, cheerful, solemn repose . . ." (284).

Once, while temporarily separated from Sophia and their children, he voiced a wish that his wife too could "now and then stand apart from thy lot, in the same manner, and behold how fair" their life was. "I think we are very happy," he mused, "—a truth that is not always so evident to me, until I step aside from our daily life." Sophia responded that, although her husband should protect himself from "the wear & tear" of domestic life, she herself did "not need to stand apart from our daily life to see how fair & blest is our lot, because it is the mother's vocation to be in the midst of little cares & great blisses."[28] Catharine Beecher, who insisted that a successful housekeeper must stand above the "minutiae of domestic arrangements" which would otherwise absorb all her attention, would have read Sophia Hawthorne's embrace of the "wear & tear" of daily domestic life as a recipe for weakmindedness.[29]

Robert K. Martin's generalizations about domesticity have little relevance to Beecher's *Treatise on Domestic Economy,* which advocates its own ethos of defamiliarization. Instead Martin's view of domestic womanhood and the homosocial constitution of the canon he supports it with subsume Hawthorne's own construction of women. Despite the momentary wavering in his letter to his wife, Nathaniel seems ultimately to have shared Sophia's perspective on women's obligation to live in the quotidian. *The Scarlet Letter* represents the ability to stand apart from daily life as a distinctly male prerogative. Hawthorne introduces Hester Prynne—or rather, the scarlet letter she is condemned to wear—as an agent of defamiliarization. As Lauren Berlant writes, "the juridical spectacle . . . situates the novel, from its very origins, in an overcoming of daily life."[30] When Hester emerges from the prison and stands before the crowd gathered in the marketplace to witness her shame,

> the point which drew all eyes, and, as it were, transfigured the wearer,—so that both men and women, who had been familiarly acquainted with Hester Prynne, were now impressed as if they beheld her for the first time,—was that SCARLET LETTER, so fantastically embroidered and illuminated upon her bosom. It had the effect of a spell, taking her out of the ordinary relations with humanity, and inclosing her in a sphere by herself. (53–54)

Hawthorne uses the letter to demarcate an opposition between "the state's theatrical and symbolic domination of the public sphere" and something "much harder to represent, the mental and physical practices of . . . personal life."[31] Hence, in chapter 5, when Hester returns home after being displayed in the marketplace as the public symbol of sin, she retreats back into privacy, into "daily custom" and the "ordinary resources of her nature," which will sustain her during more quotidian trials "[t]omorrow," "the next day," and "the next" (78–9).

Although outwardly Hester's life proceeds uneventfully, inwardly the letter continues to disrupt daily custom and ordinary relations. "Made into a stranger, she gains the stranger's ability to see the arbitrariness of signs,"[32] an ability contemporary criticism identifies as the ground of all struggle against the status quo. Hester's dedication to a revolutionary ethos ("the world's law was no law for her mind" [164]) ensues from her exile from the ordinary. At her most radical, her

> intellect and heart had their home, as it were, in desert places, where she roamed as freely as the wild Indian in his woods. . . . [S]he . . . looked from this estranged point of view at human institutions, and whatever priests or legislators had established; criticizing all with hardly more reverence than the Indian would feel for the clerical band, the judicial robe, the pillory, the gallows, the fireside, or the church. (199)

The "as it were" qualifying "home" suggests that for Hawthorne social critique demands disengagement from the familiar. Hester views society from the estranged perspective Hawthorne attributes to the "wild Indian," that is, the person who has no home and roams about at will. "There was wild and ghastly scenery all around her, and a home . . . nowhere." This "ghastly scenery" is *unheimlich* both in the sense of "unhomelike" and "uncanny." Its landscape is that of gothic romance rather than the realist novel: "Hester Prynne . . . wandered without a clew in the dark labyrinth of mind; now turned aside by an insurmountable precipice; now starting back from a deep chasm" (166).

Home is such a powerful symbol in Hawthorne's imaginative writings, notebooks, and letters because he associates it with that which is most familiar: the self. Hester's situation recalls that of Wakefield, the antihero in Hawthorne's tale of the same name, who for twenty years lives a block away from his house, contemplating the events that occur there in his absence. In both "Wakefield" (1837) and *The Scarlet Letter* home is the symbol of everyday life. Only after they have disengaged themselves from the domestic can Hawthorne's characters study it, or "awaken" to it. Like the narrator of the preface to "Rappaccini's Daughter," Wakefield is the figure of the man trying to look at himself, to see himself from the outside, to witness his own queerness.

For Hawthorne, self-estrangement constitutes male subjectivity. It also signifies a fundamental violation of female subjectivity. "Wakefield" presents its alienated and self-alienated male protagonist as "foolish" and perhaps even "mad."[33] *The Scarlet Letter,* on the other hand, suggests that the woman with access to this estranged perspective is unsexed by it. One of the "effects of the symbol" that Hester wears on her breast is that "some attribute . . . departed from her, the permanence of which had been essential to keep her a woman" (163). Radical Hester resembles the female suicide whose body Hawthorne once witnessed a team of men pull from a river. "I suppose one friend would have saved her," Hawthorne reflected on the suicide in his notebooks, "but she died for want of sympathy—a severe penalty for having cultivated and refined herself out of the sphere of her natural connections."[34]

Introduced to the reader as an object of melodramatic spectacle, Hester Prynne is gradually reassimilated into the "feminine" realm of everyday life. The aura of the letter fades, and Hester becomes "a kind of voluntary nurse" in the community, "doing whatever miscellaneous good she might; taking upon herself, likewise, to give advice in all matters, especially those of the heart" (32). Unlike Hawthorne's principle male characters, Hester not only survives her sorrows but is said to be residing just outside of Salem long after the events of the narrative have transpired—as though she had some existence independent of her textual one. Hawthorne creates the effect of realism through the illusion of self-sufficiency. Ultimately, Hawthorne refamiliarizes Hester, bringing her back within the codes of novelistic probability and back within the "miscellaneous" realm of domestic concerns ("matters of the heart").

Trouble in Criticism's Paradise of Bachelors

Regarding his acceptance of the position of Surveyor of Salem's Custom House, Hawthorne wrote:

> It is a good lesson—though it may often be a hard one—for a man who has dreamed of literary fame, and of making for himself a rank among the world's dignitaries by such means, to step aside out of the

narrow circle in which his claims are recognized, and to find how utterly devoid of significance, beyond that circle, is all that he achieves, and all that he aims at. (26–7)

This passage expresses more than simply Hawthorne's sense of dislocation in the Custom House. It also relocates within a proper, male subject (that is, Hawthorne himself) the radical Hester's ability to "step aside out of the narrow circle" of the familiar and indulge contrary opinions and values. Hawthorne further appropriates the political significance of Hester's temporary estrangement in *The Scarlet Letter* by disavowing any partisan loyalty despite his status as a Democratic Party appointee in Boston's Custom House. Thus the preface appears doubly tendentious when read in light of Hester's reinscription within the "narrow circle" of realist codes: it defines distance from the familiar as a male prerogative and recaptures for the author himself the freedom from institutions and conventions gained through Hester's defamiliarized perspective.

By the time Hawthorne wrote *The Scarlet Letter,* the familiar was increasingly associated with women, home, and realism. George Dekker writes that as early as the 1820s there was "a polar opposition" (at least in the minds of the writers of the period) "between [the novel or] a kind [of prose fiction] that faithfully mirrors familiar and contemporary experience and [the romance or a kind of prose fiction] that in various ways . . . defies or departs from the norm."[35] Moreover, by midcentury, writers, reviewers, and publishers insisted upon the difference between homey or domestic narratives and sublime art.[36]

But categories of prose narrative (like all categories founded upon a binary opposition) have no discrete existence; they possess meaning only in relation to each other. "The Custom-House" conveys the codependence of the domestic and the sublime when it depicts home as the scene of writing romance. Pressure on the language of the familiar and the strange in the discussion of romance in "The Custom-House" reveals that Hawthorne's apparent fondness for domestic scenes is in fact part of a strategy for differentiating between the "homelike" and his own aesthetic. "The Custom-House" aligns romance with the defamiliarizing effect of the aura. In a passage whose imagery and syntax anticipate that of the meteor scene, Hawthorne describes how a "dim coal-fire," partially illuminating the parlor in which he writes, transforms "the floor of our familiar room" into the "neutral territory" of

romance by defamiliarizing the everyday life represented by the contents of the room. The fire "throws its unobtrusive tinge throughout the
room, with a faint ruddiness upon the walls and ceiling, and a reflected
gleam from the polish of the furniture." This aura represents a literary
method explicitly divorced from the familiar and instead associated with
"dream[ing] *strange* things and mak[ing] them look like truth" (36, my
italics).

As in the meteor scene, the order of the *heimlich* in this passage is
designated by the hypotactic, by the details that go into conveying the
effect of realism. A list of familiar / familial objects follows Hawthorne's
declaration that "moonlight, in a familiar room . . . is a medium the
most suitable for a romance-writer": "There is the little domestic
scenery of the well-known apartment; the chairs, with each its separate
individuality; the centre-table, sustaining a work-basket, a volume or
two, and an extinguished lamp; the sofa; the book-case; the picture on
the wall . . ." These "details" are "completely seen" but "are so spir-
itualized by the unusual light, that they seem to lose their actual substance, and become things of intellect":

> Nothing is too small or too trifling to undergo this change, and
> acquire dignity thereby. A child's shoe; the doll, seated in her little
> wicker carriage; the hobby-horse;—whatever, in a word, has been
> used or played with, during the day, is now invested with a quality of
> strangeness and remoteness, though still almost as vividly present as
> by daylight. (35-6)[37]

The enumerated objects in this passage (like the ones in the meteor
scene) represent what Naomi Schor calls the "*detail as negativity*": "the
everyday, whose 'prosiness' is rooted in the domestic sphere of social life
presided over by women."[38] To define his aesthetic in opposition to the
feminine order, Hawthorne must enumerate domestic details and familiar scenes. *The Scarlet Letter* must fashion the home and its aesthetic in
order to disavow them.

In Hawthorne's aesthetics of defamiliarization we see the beginnings
of what Andreas Huyssen calls the "repudiation of *Trivialliteratur* that has
always been one of the constitutive features of a modernist aesthetic
intent on distancing itself and its products from the trivialities and
banalities of everyday life."[39] The terms of repudiation are Hawthorne's
own imaginary labors—not self-evident truths on which critics can base

their estimates of literary value. Hawthorne manufactures the familiar and scenarios of defamiliarization in order to designate the literary value of his own writing. Explaining in the preface to *The Scarlet Letter* why he did not compose a book out of his experiences in the Custom House, Hawthorne asserts that he was unable to find "the true and indestructible value that lay hidden in the petty and wearisome incidents, and ordinary characters, with which [he] was . . . conversant" while employed there. Perhaps at some point in the future, he speculates, he may put his now too-familiar experiences on paper and suddenly see them defamiliarized, "turn[ed] to gold upon the page" (37)—a formulation recalling his speculation that "in the spiritual world, the old physician and the minister . . . may, unawares, have found their earthly stock of hatred and antipathy transmuted into golden love" (260–1).

The realist quotidian represented by the author's experience in the Custom House, repudiated at some future point, will yield literary value ("gold"). Hawthorne's repudiation of realist language takes a variety of forms in his work, but at some level they all express Hawthorne's attempt to create professional currency for himself by defining literary value against a feminine realm, which he associates with Hester Prynne's quotidian afterlife, the domestic scenes from which he stages his early exclusion and later detachment, and finally the realist language he interprets as "feminine."

Hawthorne imagined that the women writers of his day lacked the capacity to overcome the petty and wearisome realm of the domestic. In a letter to his publisher William Ticknor (who also published the work of several prominent women writers), Hawthorne complained that the poetry of Julia Ward Howe "let out a whole history of domestic unhappiness" (presumably, the history of Howe's own troubled marriage).[40] Another letter states that Howe has "no genius or talent, except for making public what she ought to keep to herself."[41] Even when Hawthorne spoke well of his female competitors, he referred to their work as though it were an unmediated transcription of their private lives. According to him, the strength of Fanny Fern's semi-autobiographical *Ruth Hall* lay in its author's willingness to "throw off the restraints of decency, and come before the public stark naked, as it were."[42]

Whereas Hawthorne imagined that women's texts were scandalously underdressed records of personal experience, throughout his career he insisted upon the distance between his creative work and his private life.

Hawthorne's vision of himself as a writer "disinclined to talk overmuch of [him]self and [his] affairs at the fireside" (3) contrasts markedly with his image of women writers unable to leave the fireside or themselves. "These things hide the man, instead of displaying him," reads the preface to *The Snow-Image*.[43] "So far as I am a man of really individual attributes," he states in the preface to *Mosses from an Old Manse*, "I veil my face."[44] A letter he wrote to his wife suggests that his estranging veil represents a claim to universality for his art. There Hawthorne refers to an "involuntary reserve" on his part, which gives "objectivity" to his writing: "when people think that I am pouring myself out in a tale or essay, I am merely telling what is most common to human nature, not what is peculiar to myself."[45]

The nakedness of women writers symbolizes their inability to get away from what is peculiar to themselves. Their lack of proper attire leaves them house-bound, unsuitable for any function except the private one of sexual reproduction. Doomed to live in the domestic, they can never step back, see things "objectively," or undergo the estrangements of perspective Hawthorne demarcates as a male prerogative. Like the scenes of the defamiliarized domestic in *The Scarlet Letter*, Hawthorne's veil shields him from women's inevitable self-identity.

Yet being veiled is not exactly the opposite of being naked; male privilege comes with its own restrictions. As an image the veil has its own sexual connotations, expressed in a desire to uncover, to reveal, and to know. In the preface to *The Scarlet Letter*, Hawthorne refers to "the inmost Me behind its veil" (4), but the veil does not hide Hawthorne without also rendering him (like Dimmesdale) an object of sexualized investigation. Hawthorne's sign of male privilege comes with its own regulatory power. And Hawthorne's repudiation of homey novels does not liberate his literary imagination from compulsory heterosexuality; it leads him to author a homosocial plot expressing and provoking male sexual panic, fear of exposure, and terror in self-disclosure.

The Scarlet Letter stages the scenarios of defamiliarization by which critics recognize the text as ideologically subversive, universally significant, historically transcendent—as, in short, a modernist text. A great deal rides on the association of Hawthorne's defamiliarizing aesthetics with modernist self-reflexivity. The alliance helped transform the literature of the nineteenth-century United States into a legitimate field for academic study. "Preference for self-reflexive (romance and symbolistic) form," notes one critic, "is stressed in twentieth-century accounts of the American Renaissance."[46] As Gerald Graff points out, since World War I literary critics have "tended to believe that the project of cultural politics is to undermine all 'bourgeois' perceptual, artistic, and philosophical categories, which allegedly prop up authoritarianism." This has resulted in the widespread conviction "that formalist art and self-reflexive writing are more fundamentally subversive than critical realisms." Graff concludes that the "highest expression [of self-reflexivity] defines for many critics the classic American literary tradition," and he includes in this generalization even very contemporary critics who have rewritten "the Americanness of American literature" in the "deconstructionist register [of] reflexive awareness of the problematic of writing itself."[47]

Through his scenes of defamiliarization Hawthorne relived the paradise of bachelors at Augusta. The homosocial canon of the American Renaissance represents another means of reliving a fantasy of freedom from society. But, like Hawthorne's paradise, this premodernist canon *is* troubled by "restrictions of society," against which it is defined. Critics will not discern the trouble in paradise until they begin to read the antebellum figures of self-identical womanhood and alienated manhood as textual productions.

Hawthorne in fact expended a great deal of creative effort in making estrangement a male province, a symbol of radicalism, and the basis of literary hierarchy: strange things which now look like truth. Critical celebrations of the modernism of mid-century "classics" ignore Hawthorne's labor, presenting his optic shifts as the truth—rather than a trope—of demystification, a trope which embeds its figures of familiarity and transcendence within protocols of gender and sexuality.

CONCLUSION

Robert K. Martin identifies estrangement as the basis of Hawthorne's aesthetic radicalism. But, adds Martin, "estrangement . . . was foreclosed to most American women of Hawthorne's time, who were increasingly bound to the familiar limitations of the domestic."[1] As an echo of Hawthorne's own attempt to make defamiliarization and social critique the province of the male writer, Martin's statement exemplifies the problem with contemporary critical treatments of domesticity described throughout this book: the repeated reinscription of the antebellum period's gendered figures of hegemony and resistance.

As my reading of Hawthorne shows, the antebellum creation of gendered political meaning informs even the premodernist aesthetics on which critics base many of their claims for the subversiveness of American Renaissance texts. *The Scarlet Letter*'s aesthetics of perspectival insecurity require that Hawthorne first secure the domestic as a symbol of a familiarity and self-identity which only men can transcend. Hawthorne's optic shifts do not just unsettle meaning; they also produce power by making male homosocial cultural authority coterminous with doubt and anxiety over male sexual identity.

Despite references to the impact of social roles created by domesticity, critics' characterization of women's culture do not actually historicize the significance of the distinctions they draw between men's and women's literary expression. Instead they reiterate gender difference as canonical male authors invested it with political significance: as a way of proclaiming the oppositional status of manhood in an age of putatively "feminine" modernity. Domesticity serves a crucial role in articulations of the canon because its organization of a myriad of social and cultural categories into versions of the categorical difference between the genders still has utility for criticism dedicated to defining the literary in terms of opposition (to convention, to ideology, to power). The invocation of separate spheres endows critical binarisms like hegemonic/ subversive with the "obviousness" of gender difference and inhibits investigation of the oppositional logic supporting our understanding of cultural politics. The critical binarisms generated as evidence of gendered political difference remain infinitely more stable if critics refrain from reading critiques of domesticity as texts: as complex representational systems through which the antebellum period interpreted itself and not transparent renderings of a reality of (self-)alienated men and (self-)identical women.

The resistance to reading the domestic woman's cultural regime as an ideological artifact generated by "classic" texts requires analysis both as an issue of gender politics and as a reaction to the increasing access to education, literacy, and the means of cultural production which the rise of modern mass culture indicates. This access, though distributed unevenly, was not limited to middle-class women. Yet the "feminization" of early nineteenth-century cultural production and consumption is one of the most basic assumptions made by critics about the period, even in the face of dubious literary historical evidence. Representing the masses as feminine obscures the way in which constructions of countercultural authorship maintain not just male authority but also the cultural authority of a small number of male authors in the face of increasing cultural access to literacy across a range of antebellum populations.

Andreas Huyssen asserts that mass culture is "always already inscribed into the articulation of aesthetic modernism," and he argues that modernism figures mass culture in terms of an undifferentiated and passive femininity.[2] Domesticity is the particular representative of this feminine mass culture inscribed into articulations of the aesthetic modernism of the American Renaissance. Any study of the culture of the period must recognize: the impact of the antebellum grammar of gender on twentieth-century constructions of the literary as a category; the way that criticism uses it to designate countercultural expression as the prerogative of an elite group of authors exemplifying a particular aesthetics; and how both processes inhibit acknowledgement of the many fronts on which antebellum culture exerted power and voiced resistance.

Chapter 1's survey of women's writing dislodges assertions of the
political uniformity of the culture of domesticity and its ability to produce mindless conformity. Analysis of women's varied textual production reveals multiple bases for cultural resistance in the period, including those performed *through* domesticity. The critical process of making
domestic fiction into the "other" of canonical male fiction has trained
contemporary readers to imagine women's culture marching across the
antebellum period in a single formation; at the same time it has prepared
us to assume that any progressive form of cultural expression must take
the form of transcendent authorial critique of the status quo—which
this criticism distills into a critique of domesticity.

By organizing cultural politics into a battle between thoroughly transcendent and thoroughly interpellated authorial subjects, gender difference makes the literary-political difference attributed to male authors
appear more obvious than it really is. Chapter 1 argues that antebellum
masculinist resistance does not fundamentally upset the gendered logic
of domesticity. Because the work of male canonical authors has been
regarded as "virtually the opposite" of that of the women writers of the
time, critics have failed to see domestic discourse exerting anything
except a negative influence on the male "classics." I have included
canonical texts by men in this study to demonstrate that their critiques
of antebellum women's culture are themselves far too implicated in
domesticity's organization of reality into gendered domains to constitute an "alternative world" outside of it. Thus, rather than offering a
reading of antebellum culture neatly bifurcated according to oppositions
elaborated through the antebellum grammar of gender, this book has
presented domesticity's integral presence in a plurality of traditions:
mass cultural and elite, popular and marginal, women's and men's.

Disputing critical delineations of the alternative status of the classics
does not provide further evidence for the familiar thesis that middle-
class women "controlled" their society through the discourse of the
home. Domesticity does not guarantee any particular textual politics
once we cease to read it as a stable marker of difference between the
abstractly conceived categories of hegemonic and countercultural. In
fact, as the reading of Cooper's masculinist rebellion in chapter 2 shows,
both critical and fictional attempts to center questions of textual politics
upon gender conflicts surrounding the middle-class home conceal other

axes of struggle (Anglo-Native relations, in Cooper's case) represented through the language of the domestic.

Although chapter 2 raises specific questions about Foucault's understanding of modernity and about the way that New Historicism has applied it, I have nevertheless found his general interpretive model of micropolitical analysis indispensable for an alternative reading of antebellum cultural politics. Foucault posits that "there is not, on the one side, a discourse of power, and opposite it, another discourse that runs counter to it." And he explains:

> we must not imagine a world of discourse divided between . . . the dominant discourse and the dominated one; but . . . a multiplicity of discursive elements that can come into play in various strategies. It is this distribution that we must reconstruct . . . with the variants and different effects—according to who is speaking, his position of power, the institutional context in which he happens to be situated—that it implies; and with the shifts and reutilizations of identical formulas for contrary objectives. . . . Discourses are not once and for all subservient to power or raised up against it. . . . We must make allowance for the complex and unstable process whereby discourse can be both an instrument and an effect of power, but also a hindrance, a stumbling-block, a point of resistance and a starting point for an opposing strategy.[3]

Thus the question chapters 2 through 5 ask is: how do texts deploy domesticity in specific historical contexts in order to intervene a plurality of nineteenth-century power relations and what are the consequences of these various deployments for these different relations?

Chapters 2 through 5 target different platforms of antebellum struggle: the frontier, nationalist activism, bio-political reform, and cultural production. Domesticity appears at these sites not because textual endorsement or renunciation reveals the key for understanding which authors subvert and which reproduce the status quo, but rather because, as a critique of the patriarchal family, domesticity offered authors a rich and pliable symbolism for representing power and resistance. It had an affinity with languages depicting other kinds of social subordination and hence interpretive currency not only for narrations of the middle-class home but also for other contested arenas in the culture. For both its antebellum detractors and proponents, the language of domesticity helped make these conflicts representable; however, their conviction in the unbridgeable opposition between the genders means that gender's surplus of binary energies structures other categorical distinctions formed in these texts.

The security of the gender binarism in domesticity and its usefulness for mapping moral, social, and political oppositions as gender difference has had an enduring impact on how critics understand antebellum cultural politics. Critics must begin treating the dyadic confrontation of power and resistance that the doctrine of separate spheres builds into these representations of conflict with more skepticism than they have in the past.

This want of skepticism is as evident in feminist criticism as it is in renderings of the traditional canon. In resuscitating the legacy of domesticity, first-wave feminism interpreted domesticity's critique of patriarchy as evidence of the generalized oppositionality of Anglo-American women's culture. By virtue of their seclusion in the home from the male world of power, this criticism asserts, women secured insight from the margins of their society into injustices it perpetuated in the name of the patriarch.

A text like *Uncle Tom's Cabin* paves the way for contemporary feminist interpretation. Stowe can translate her hygienist domesticity into abolitionist critique because she makes power uniform and centralized by referring all its manifestations back to the patriarch. Whether oppression victimizes middle-class wives and daughters, the working class, or Southern slaves it is essentially patriarchal in origins—primary, secondary or tertiary impositions of the law of "the father who forbids" (to use Foucault's phrase). Thus figured, the power Stowe imagines is both homogeneous, "varying in scale alone," and negative, "a power to say no; in no condition to produce, capable only of posting limits . . . basically anti-energy." Foucault notes that this way of conceiving of power "render[s] what it dominates incapable of doing anything . . . except for what this power allows it to do."[4]

Domesticity's own language of critique prepares feminism to interpret any act of cultural contestation as an abridgement of power in toto. Because the centralized and deductive conception of power they assume allows only capitulation or transcendence, first-wave feminist critics had to promote domestic fiction to the subversive status formerly monopolized by the "classics" when they found signs of antipatriarchal critique and attempts to rearrange the social order in women's texts. Chapter 4 problematizes this promotion by reading Stowe's domesticity within the history of bio-politics. The social authority middle-class women gained through their particular enunciation of antipatriarchal critique gave them access to unofficial or fledgling institutions (publishing, alternative medicine, education, and social reform movements). This access, along with the class privileges which no doubt aided in their achievement, compromises antebellum women writers' status as strangers to the exercise of power; however, as I stress in that chapter, it is only if we accept Stowe's definition of power as essentially patriarchal that tracing connections between her hygienic domesticity and new power relations investing the home through discourses of reform will expose her work as simply a reproduction of the patriarchal status quo. Moreover, only if we conceive of power as a "a duality extending from the top down" will gains in access, authority, and expertise necessarily translate into middle-class women's cultural dominance.[5]

The gains clearly placed them in relationships of power to populations targeted by reform movements, but that very real power nevertheless rested on rudimentary institutional bases and was constantly preempted and circumscribed by male authority with greater institutional re-sources and leverage. First-wave feminism's binary and centralized models cannot describe the admixture of power and disenfranchisement required for analyzing the politics of domestic culture. Neither can they account for effective critiques of inequalities which emanate from within power relations—hence feminist criticism's need to overlook the class and racial prerogatives underwriting the "alternative" world of the domestic.

Because of the stress it places on disjunctions between gender analysis and racial and class hierarchies, criticism on African American women writers and domesticity is better positioned to advance micropolitical models of interpreting antebellum cultural politics. These critics voice a much-needed critique of first-wave feminism. Unfortunately, it comes at the cost of reviving the image of mystified feminine masses, sub-missively reproducing through the culture of domesticity the ideology responsible for preserving all of the most conservative aspects of their society—including patriarchal oppression of white, middle-class women. In Carby's influential reading, African American women writers borrow the form of domestic fiction in order to communicate their radical message but jettison domestic values through subtle parody and hidden critique. Carby's approach ends up mirroring many of the terms of modernist critical statements on the classics because her conception of power is centralized and unitary. It is as though in order to make power struggles between women in the integrated abolitionist movement visible, Carby must show us the forbidding father figure behind domesticity, whispering his edicts in the white woman's ear, edicts which only a marginal tradition can decipher as such.

By contrast chapter 3 argues for the utility of Anglo-American domesticity for Maria Stewart, who appears to have recognized in it a means of promoting African American women's leadership in an activist movement that defined resistance in terms of masculinist nationalism. Although the chapter disorganizes terms like "dominant" and "marginal," stressing the critical contents of domesticity in the realm of gender, it does not curtail investigations into asymmetrical power relations between Anglo-American and African American women writers. To the contrary, ignoring Anglo-American domesticity's antipatriarchal potential and defining domesticity as a limit to thought, as hegemonic censorship and self-censorship, tends to realign crucial nonalignments between the political interests, goals, and circumstances of African American and Anglo-American women writers. It leads us to conclude that if white women had possessed the wherewithal to challenge patriarchy then all of the other forms of inequality present in antebellum society that radiate outward from the patriarch's word would unravel in the process. Anglo-American women's failure to overcome specific social hierarchies of race and class is not a symptom of capitulation to power in general; it should instead function as an incentive for thinking about power and resistance as operating within specific social domains and requiring different strategies and responses within those domains.

The difference between "dominant" and "marginal" discourses needs to be conceived in terms other than opposition between passive and active. Ideological dissemination works by inciting activity, not deadening it; however, the consequences of incitement produce unforeseen implementations, as they are integrated into discontinuous fields of power relations. My reading of Stewart demonstrates that no one group owns domesticity. Stewart manages to communicate a much more radical agenda of race and class critique than the Anglo-American writers included in this study because her circumstances of articulation are radically different and because a discourse of black nationalism provides a matrix of intelligibility for her domesticity absent from other antebellum communities. And if, as I speculate, even for an intellectual as inventive as Stewart domesticity may have helped write an early ending to her career as a public speaker, we should take this as a sign of another kind of nonalignment: one between resistance and transcendence. Stewart did not fail by investing in domesticity; analysis of cultural politics fails her by requiring authorial transcendence as evidence of resistance.

Feminist and African American critical readings of domesticity have provided astute analyses of the politics of canon formation. My own study, is, of course, indebted to this work. *Home Fronts,* however, represents a substantially different approach. It shifts attention onto the fundamental definitions of power and resistance operating in our calculations of cultural politics and offers a method for estimating the political value of cultural expression that defies traditional constructions of the literary as transcendence.

❧ NOTES

Introduction

1   Richard H. Brodhead, *The School of Hawthorne* (New York: Oxford University Press, 1986), 20.

2   Myra Jehlen, "Archimedes and the Paradox of Feminist Criticism," *Signs* 6 (Summer 1981), 593.

3   Jane Tompkins, *Sensational Designs: The Cultural Work of American Fiction, 1790–1860* (New York: Oxford University Press, 1985), 124, 144. Helen Waite Papashvily advanced an early argument for the countercultural status of women's domestic fiction in *All the Happy Endings: A Study of the Domestic Novel in America* (New York: Harper and Brothers, 1956), xiii–xvii.

4   Laura Wexler, "Tender Violence: Literary Eavesdropping, Domestic Fiction, and Educational Reform," in *The Culture of Sentiment: Race, Gender, and Sentimentality in 19th Century America,* ed. Shirley Samuels (New York: Oxford University Press, 1992), 15.

5   Hazel V. Carby, *Reconstructing Womanhood: The Emergence of the Afro-American Woman Novelist* (New York: Oxford University Press, 1987), 58, 50, 49.

6   Herman Melville, "Hawthorne and His Mosses," in *The Piazza Tales and Other Prose Pieces 1839–1860,* ed. Harrison Hayford, et al. (Evanston and Chicago: Northwestern University Press and The Newberry Library, 1987), 249, 250, 251.

7   Michel Foucault, *The History of Sexuality: An Introduction,* trans. Robert Hurley (New York: Vintage, 1980), 95–96. Henceforth quotations from *The History of Sexuality* will be taken from this edition and cited parenthetically.

8   Cherríe Moraga, *Loving in the War Years: Lo que nunca pasó por sus labios* (Boston: South End Press, 1983), 108.

9   Ann Cvetkovich's *Mixed Feelings: Feminism, Mass Culture, and Victorian Sensationalism* (New Brunswick: Rutgers University Press, 1992) contemplates similar interpretive problems raised by British Victorian women's fiction for Marxist feminism.

Chapter 1   A Society Controlled by Women: An Overview

1   H. Ross Brown, *The Sentimental Novel in America, 1789–1860* (Durham, N.C.:
    Duke University Press, 1940), 281.

2   Cf. Joanne Dobson's statement that a "reenvisioned" American Renaissance will
    issue from "the current movement toward inclusion of women's literature in our
    literary history." See her essay, "The American Renaissance Reenvisioned," in
    The (Other) American Traditions: Nineteenth-Century Women Writers, ed. Joyce War-
    ren (New Brunswick, N.J.: Rutgers University Press, 1993), 165. Other femi-
    nist readings of U.S. literary history upon which my chapter draws are: Jane
    Tompkins, *Sensational Designs: The Cultural Work of American Fiction, 1790–1860*
    (New York: Oxford University Press, 1985), xi–xix, 3–39; Joyce W. Warren,
    "Introduction: Canon and Canon Fodder," in Warren, ed., 1–25; Nina Baym,
    "Melodramas of Beset Manhood," in *Feminism and American Literary History: Essays*
    (New Brunswick, N.J.: Rutgers University Press, 1992), 3–18; and my own
    essay "Domesticity and Novels," in *The Columbia History of the American Novel,* ed.
    Emory Elliott (New York: Columbia University Press, 1991), 110–29.

3   James Fenimore Cooper, *The Spy: A Tale of the Neutral Ground* (New Haven,
    Conn.: College and University Press, 1971), 33.

4   The comment appears in a letter Hawthorne wrote to his publisher on 19 January
    1855 and is published in *The Letters, 1853–1856,* vol. XVII of *The Centenary Edition
    of the Works of Nathaniel Hawthorne* (Columbus: Ohio State University Press,
    1987), 303–5.

5   Ann Douglas, *The Feminization of American Culture* (New York: Avon Books,
    1977), 275. Henceforth, quotations from Douglas's book will be taken from the
    1977 edition and cited parenthetically, but readers should also consult Douglas's
    new Preface to *The Feminization of American Culture* (New York: Anchor Books,
    1988), xi–xiv, for her response to critiques of canon-formation conducted in the
    last decade.

6   David S. Reynolds, *Beneath the American Renaissance: The Subversive Imagination in
    the Age of Emerson and Melville* (Cambridge: Harvard University Press, 1989),
    337–38.

7   Cathy N. Davidson, *Revolution and the Word: The Rise of the Novel in America* (New
    York: Oxford University Press, 1986), 98. In a note at the end of *Women's Fiction:
    A Guide to Novels by and about Women in America, 1820–1870* (Ithaca, N.Y.: Cornell
    University Press, 1978), Nina Baym warns that "in the present state of research
    into popular literature [assessments of biographers and scholars] are necessarily
    provisional":

    > Many statements about sales and reputation are offered in the scholarship
    > without adequate documentation; it would appear that most numerical esti-
    > mates are in fact educated guesses or impressionistic conclusions based on a
    > variety of sources of differing specificity and reliability. The problem is fur-
    > ther complicated by the lack of a consistent measurement of popularity . . .
    > (300)

8 Elsewhere, to back up claims that "[m]iddle-class women became in a very real sense consumers of literature" and constituted the primary readership for domestic novels (72), Douglas cites Carl Bode's *American Culture* (Carbondale and Edwardsville: Southern Illinois University Press, 1959), 109ff., and Norman F. Cantor and Michael S. Werthman, eds., *The History of Popular Culture* (New York: The Macmillan Company, 1968), 84–94. There is no mention of the gender composition of the antebellum reading audience in either of these locations; in fact, Bode writes in a later chapter that "the audience for the domestic novel was male and female both" (170).

9 William Charvat, *The Profession of Authorship in America, 1800–1870* (Columbus: Ohio State University Press, 1968), 305–6. Although Charvat declares that "the signs are many that by mid-century most of the consumers of imaginative literature were women of the upper and middle classes," the only signs he offers are contemporaneous (and generally acerbic) quips to that effect (242).

10 According to Reynolds,

> [T]he only time that female-authored American volumes had anything close to a numerical parity with male-authored ones was during the earliest stage of American fiction, between 1784 and 1810, when 41 percent of all volumes were written by women and 44 percent by men (the remaining volumes were published anonymously). By the 1830–60 period the proportion of male volumes had risen to 57 percent. These statistics reveal a notable drop in proportion to volumes written by women. It should also be noted that the sentimental-domestic fiction that is thought to have conquered the popular market actually ran a distant second to more sensational genres. (338)

11 Lucy M. Freibert and Barbara A. White, eds., *Hidden Hands: An Anthology of American Women Writers, 1790–1870* (New Brunswick, N.J.: Rutgers University Press, 1988), xii. Freibert and White base their conclusions on Frank Luther Mott's "Over-All Best Sellers in the United States," Appendix A in *Golden Multitudes: The Story of Best Sellers in the United States* (New York: The Macmillan Company, 1947), 303–15.

12 On the relationship between female authors and the male book-publishing industry, see Susan Coultrap-McQuin, *Doing Literary Business: American Women Writers in the Nineteenth Century* (Chapel Hill: University of North Carolina Press, 1990).

13 As evidence, Fred Lewis Pattee's statement that "the great mass of the American readers, for the most part women, did not think at all" comes to mind. It appears in his *The Feminine Fifties* (New York: D. Appleton-Century Company, 1940), 307.

14 On republican motherhood and other Revolutionary-era anticipations of domesticity, see Linda K. Kerber, *Women of the Republic: Intellect and Ideology in Revolutionary America* (Chapel Hill: University of North Carolina Press, 1980), 185–231; Mary Beth Norton, *Liberty's Daughters: The Revolutionary Experience of American Women, 1750–1800* (Boston and Toronto: Little, Brown and Company, 1980), 242–55; and Nancy F. Cott, *The Bonds of Womanhood: "Woman's Sphere" in*

New England, 1780–1835 (New Haven, Conn.: Yale University Press, 1977), 63–100.

15   Quoted in Barbara J. Berg, *The Remembered Gate: Origins of American Feminism* (New York: Oxford University Press, 1978), 68.

16   Quoted in T. Walter Herbert, *Dearest Beloved: The Hawthornes and the Making of the Middle-Class Family* (Berkeley and Los Angeles: University of California Press, 1993), 14.

17   Sarah J. Hale, "Conversazione," *Godey's Lady's Book* 1 (January 1837), 1–2. Quoted in David Leverenz, *Manhood in the American Renaissance* (Ithaca, N.Y.: Cornell University Press, 1989), 148. Sarah J. Hale, *Godey's Ladies' Magazine* 1 (1828), 422–3. Quoted in Douglas, 86.

18   Lydia Maria Child, *The Mother's Book* (1831; reprint New York: Arno Press and The New York Times, 1972), 90–1.

19   Maria Susanna Cummins, *The Lamplighter* (New Brunswick, N.J.: Rutgers University Press, 1988), 66–7.

20   Cf. Douglas's discussion of the connections between the doctrine of female influence and women's literary vocation on pages 50–93. Nevertheless, it should be acknowledged that writing's status as a "private" enterprise appropriate for women was conventional rather than inevitable. Mary Kelley points this out in her book *Private Woman, Public Stage: Literary Domesticity in Nineteenth-Century America* (New York: Oxford University Press, 1984). In a collection entitled *Woman and Her Needs* (1851; reprinted in *Liberating the Home* [New York: Arno Press, 1974]), nineteenth-century women's rights advocate and novelist Elizabeth Oakes Smith undermines this view of writing. She quotes contemptuously from the work of one Mrs. S. C. Hall, who asserted that woman is happiest when *"enshrined in the privacy of domestic love and domestic duty, so perfectly is she constituted for the cares, the affections, the duties, the blessed duties of unpublic life."* To this Smith responds:

> If Mrs. S. C. Hall really thought this—really believed that a human being is happier for holding the greater part of its nature in abeyance, she ought herself never to have written—she should have buried her fine talents, and shut out from her eyes all the freshness and freedom of vision which help to make our life a well-spring of happiness. (87)

21   Nathaniel Hawthorne, *The Scarlet Letter,* in vol. I of *The Centenary Edition of the Works of Nathaniel Hawthorne* (Columbus: Ohio State University Press, 1962), 50.

22   Harriet Beecher Stowe, *The Pearl of Orr's Island: A Story of the Coast of Maine* (1862; reprint New York: AMS, 1967), 149, 163.

23   Leverenz, 172, 179.

24   Cf. Sacvan Bercovitch's term, "cultural symbology," which he uses to describe the "[highly volatile] system of symbolic meanings that encompasses text and context alike, simultaneously nourishing the imagination and marking its boundaries." See Bercovitch's *The Office of the Scarlet Letter* (Baltimore, Md.: Johns Hopkins University Press, 1991), xvii.

25 Mary Poovey, *Uneven Developments: The Ideological Work of Gender in Mid-Victorian England* (Chicago: University of Chicago Press, 1988), 3.

26 Cf. Barbara Leslie Epstein's statement in *The Politics of Domesticity: Women, Evangelism, and Temperance in Nineteenth-Century America* (Middletown, Conn.: Wesleyan University Press, 1981) that domestic writers like Catharine Beecher

> can[not] be dismissed as the victims of false consciousness. In large historical perspective, domesticity represented a weakening of women's power in relation to men, but in an immediate sense, it represented the best of all available alternatives; and by providing women with a role that was clearly defined and widely venerated, it offered them an arena for self-development and a base from which to press their claims. (84)

27 Jean-Jacques Rousseau, *Émile or On Education,* trans. Allan Bloom (New York: Basic Books, 1979), 365.

28 Hannah More, *Strictures on the Modern System of Female Education,* 3rd American ed. (Boston: Joseph Bumstead, 1802), 40.

29 Eliza Buckminster Lee, *Parthenia: or, The Last Days of Paganism* (Boston: Ticknor and Fields, 1858), 93–4.

30 Harriet Beecher Stowe, *Uncle Tom's Cabin; or Life Among the Lowly* (Boston: J. P. Jewett, 1852), vol. 1, 120.

31 Harriet Beecher Stowe, *Oldtown Folks* (1869; reprint New Brunswick, N.J.: Rutgers University Press, 1987), 387, 319.

32 Harriet Beecher Stowe, *The Minister's Wooing* (1859; reprint New York: AMS, 1967), 29.

33 Stowe, *The Pearl of Orr's Island,* 391.

34 Rousseau, 373.

35 More, 61.

36 Catharine E. Beecher, *Letters to the People on Health and Happiness* (New York: Harper and Brothers, 1855), 109.

37 Louisa May Alcott, *Little Women* (New York: Modern Library, 1983), 9–10.

38 Louisa May Alcott, *Behind a Mask; or a Woman's Power* in *Alternative Alcott,* ed. Elaine Showalter (New Brunswick, N.J.: Rutgers University Press, 1988), 106.

39 Alcott, *Little Women,* 7, 10, 16.

40 See Douglas, 81.

41 Harriet Beecher Stowe to James Fields, 27 October [1863], Fields Papers, Huntington Library. Quoted in Joan D. Hedrick, *Harriet Beecher Stowe: A Life* (New York: Oxford University Press, 1994), 312.

42 Child, 9.

43 Horace Bushnell, *Christian Nurture* (1847; reprint New Haven, Conn.: Yale University Press, 1947), 7.

44 Nancy Armstrong, *Desire and Domestic Fiction: A Political History of the Novel* (New York: Oxford University Press, 1987), 66.

45 Lydia Maria Child, *Hobomok and Other Writings on Indians,* ed. Carolyn L. Karcher (New Brunswick, N.J.: Rutgers University Press, 1986), 48.

46   Catharine Maria Sedgwick, *Hope Leslie; or Early Times in the Massachusetts* (New Brunswick, N.J.: Rutgers University Press, 1987), 123, 16, 153, 123. For a thorough treatment of the complexities of Sedgwick's identification of white women and natives, consult Dana Nelson, *The Word in Black and White: Reading "Race" in American Culture* (New York: Oxford University Press, 1992), 65–89.

47   Harriet E. Wilson, *Our Nig; or, Sketches from the Life of a Free Black* (New York: Vintage Books, 1983), 127, 46.

48   Claudia Tate, *Domestic Allegories of Political Desire: The Black Heroine's Text at the Turn of the Century* (New York: Oxford University Press, 1992), 91.

49   In *Our Nig*'s preface Wilson requests the "patronage" of her "colored brethren." Barbara A. White comments on the significance of this appeal in " 'Our Nig' and the She-Devil: New Information about Harriet Wilson and the 'Bellmont' Family," *American Literature* 65 (March 1993): 19–52.

50   Maria W. Stewart, "Religion and the Pure Principles of Morality," in *Maria W. Stewart: America's First Black Woman Political Writer: Essays and Speeches,* ed. Marilyn Richardson (Bloomington and Indianapolis: Indiana University Press, 1987), 37, 68.

51   Nell Irvin Painter also remarks on similarities between Stewart's and Truth's speeches in "Difference, Slavery, and Memory: Sojourner Truth in Feminist Abolitionism," in *The Abolitionist Sisterhood: Women's Political Culture in Antebellum America,* ed. Jean Fagan Yellin and John C. Van Horne (Ithaca, N.Y.: Cornell University Press, 1994), 139–58.

52   [Olive Gilbert and Frances W. Titus,] *Narrative of Sojourner Truth* (1878; reprint Salem: Ayer, 1992), 194 my italics, 198.

53   Tate, 133, 134.

54   Anna Julia Cooper, *A Voice from the South* (New York: Oxford University Press, 1988), 28–31. Quoted in Joyce Hope Scott, "From Foreground to Margin: Female Configuration and Masculine Self-Representation in Black Nationalist Fiction" in *Nationalisms and Sexualities,* ed. Andrew Parker, Mary Russo, Doris Sommer, and Patricia Yaeger (New York: Routledge Press, 1992), 299.

55   Scott, 299.

56   Elizabeth Keckley, *Behind the Scenes; Or, Thirty Years a Slave, and Four Years in the White House* (New York: Oxford University Press, 1988), 144–6.

57   Smith, 23, 103, 16–7, 90.

58   Dorothy Berkson, " 'So We All Became Mothers': Harriet Beecher Stowe, Charlotte Perkins Gilman, and the New World of Women's Culture," in *Feminism, Utopia, and Narrative,* ed. Libby Falk Jones and Sarah Webster Goodwin (Knoxville: University of Tennessee Press, 1990), 101.

59   Cott, 201, 155.

60   L. H. Sigourney, *Letters to Mothers,* 2nd ed. (New York: Harper and Brothers, 1839), 14.

61   For more on racism in the early suffrage movement, see Ellen Carol DuBois, *Feminism and Suffrage: The Emergence of an Independent Women's Movement in America, 1848–1869* (Ithaca, N.Y.: Cornell University Press, 1978).

62 Poovey, 3.

63 Louisa May Alcott, *Work: A Story of Experience* (New York: Arno Press, 1977), 1–2.

64 Mary J. Studley, *What Our Girls Ought to Know* (New York: M. L. Holbrook and Company, 1878), 9. My understanding of the relationship between women's medicine and domesticity is indebted to Martha H. Verbrugge's, *Able-Bodied Womanhood: Personal Health and Social Change in Nineteenth-Century Boston* (New York: Oxford University Press, 1988) and Regina Markell Morantz-Sanchez's *Sympathy and Science: Women Physicians in American Medicine* (New York: Oxford University Press, 1985).

65 Elizabeth Blackwell, "The Influence of Women in the Profession of Medicine" (1889), 28; "The Religion of Health" (1871), 243–4. Both essays are reprinted in Blackwell's *Essays in Medical Sociology,* vol. 2 (1902; reprint New York: Arno Press, 1972).

66 Katherine Kish Sklar, "The Historical Foundations of Women's Power in the Creation of the American Welfare State, 1830–1930," in *Mothers of a New World: Maternalist Politics and the Origins of Welfare States,* ed. Seth Koven and Sonya Michel (New York: Routledge, 1993), 61.

67 Koven and Michel, "Mother Worlds," Introduction to Koven and Michel, 4.

68 See Jacques Donzelot, *The Policing of Families,* trans. Robert Hurley (New York: Pantheon Books, 1979), xxiv–xxvii.

Chapter 2 *Vanishing Americans: James Fenimore Cooper*

1 Brian W. Dippie, *The Vanishing American: White Attitudes and U.S. Indian Policy* (Middletown, Conn.: Wesleyan University Press, 1982), 2. Dippie borrows the phrase from G. Harrison Orians, *The Cult of the Vanishing American: A Century View* (Toledo, Ohio: H. J. Chittenden, 1934). Reading William P. Kelly's discussion of *The Last of the Mohicans* in *Plotting America's Past: Fenimore Cooper and The Leatherstocking Tales* (Carbondale, Ill.: Southern University Press, 1983), 45–84, initially suggested to me several of the themes which this chapter pursues.

2 James Fenimore Cooper, *The Last of the Mohicans; A Narrative of 1757* (Albany: State University of New York Press, 1983), 6–7. Hereafter quotations will be taken from this edition and cited parenthetically in the text.

3 In fact, the rise of the cult of the Vanishing American corresponds roughly with the rise of the U.S. government's policy of Indian Removal, a massive military campaign of systematic dispossession and effective extermination begun in the late 1820s. According to Francis Paul Prucha in *The Great Father: The United States Government and the American Indians* (Lincoln: University of Nebraska Press, 1984), "The military phase of Indian relations" would not end until the early 1880s (560). Thus we see just how much effort went into effecting the "inevitable."

4 The figure of the falling native has endured well into the twentieth century. My grandfather, who worked as an extra in Hollywood during the Depression and

who claimed to have played a Mohican in the original film version of *The Last of the Mohicans,* used to joke about how all he did as an actor in that movie was to be shot off of horses. Contemporary Chippewa writer Louise Erdrich parodies that popular cultural representation of Indians in her novel *Love Medicine* (New York: Harper, 1984). Her character Nector Kashpaw, whose career in Hollywood westerns has consisted exclusively in falling off horses, comments that "death was the extent of Indian acting in the movie theater" (90). He also poses for a white artist's painting called "The Plunge of the Brave," about which he says:

> There I was, jumping off a cliff, naked of course, down into a rock river. Certain death. Remember Custer's saying? The only good Indian is a dead Indian? Well from my dealings with whites I would add to that quote: "The only interesting Indian is dead, or dying by falling backwards off a horse." (91)

I thank Jackie Henkel for directing me to this passage in Erdrich's novel.

5   Amariah Brigham, *Remarks on the Influence of Mental Cultivation and Mental Excitement Upon Health,* 2nd ed. (1833; reprint New York: Arno Press, 1973), 49, 42, 36, 45.

6   Margaret Fuller, *Summer on the Lakes, in 1843* (Boston: Charles C. Little and James Brown; New York: Charles S. Francis, 1844), 221, 182.

7   Brigham, vii, viii.

8   For a relevant discussion of the intersecting rhetorics of domesticity and imperialism, see Amy Kaplan, "Romancing the Empire: The Embodiment of American Masculinity in the Popular Historical Novel of the 1890s," *American Literary History* 2 (Winter 1990): 659–90.

9   Catharine E. Beecher, *Letters to the People on Health and Happiness* (New York: Harper and Brothers, 1855), 8, 10, 8.

10   The criticism on the Leatherstocking tales has played a crucial role in establishing for us a sense of ideological distance between the frontier and the home in the nineteenth-century United States. Since D. H. Lawrence's famous analysis of Cooper's Leatherstocking series appeared in 1923, Cooper criticism has taken as one of its perennial themes the antifeminine (if not outright misogynist) sensibility compelling Natty Bumppo's flight from the civilized society of women into the savage society of the red man. See, for example, Lawrence's *Studies in Classic American Literature* (Garden City, New York: Doubleday, 1951) and Leslie A. Fiedler's *Love and Death in the American Novel* (Cleveland, Ohio and New York: Meridian, 1960).

11   Michel Foucault, *The History of Sexuality, Volume I: An Introduction,* trans. Robert Hurley (New York: Vintage, 1980), 147.

12   Foucault, 136–7, 146.

13   Ibid., 59.

14   D. A. Miller, *The Novel and the Police* (Berkeley and Los Angeles: University of California Press, 1988), viii.

15   Freud writes: "In inverted types, a predominance of archaic constitutions and primitive psychical mechanisms is regularly to be found." See "The Sexual Aber-

rations," in *Three Essays on the Theory of Sexuality,* trans. and revised James Strachey (New York: Basic Books, 1962), p. 12.

16 Beecher, 8.

17 Jean-Jacques Rousseau, *Émile or On Education,* trans. Allan Bloom (New York: Basic Books, 1979), 215, 216, 165.

18 Fiedler, 189.

19 Henry David Thoreau, *Walden,* in *Walden and Civil Disobedience,* ed. Owen Thomas (New York: Norton, 1966), 68, 72, 68.

20 Ibid., 67 (my italics), 68 (my italics), 70, 68, 71.

21 "Momism" is Rogin's term for a "demonic version of domestic ideology" that expresses anxiety over the "maternal power generated by domesticity." Whereas Rogin discusses momism as a twentieth-century response to the revival of the domestic ideal in the 1950s, I am suggesting that domesticity and its demonic double arose simultaneously in the antebellum period and were mutually reinforcing. See Michael Paul Rogin, *Ronald Reagan, The Movie and Other Episodes in Political Demonology* (Berkeley: University of California Press, 1987), 242.

22 Hannah More, *Strictures on the Modern System of Female Education,* 3rd American ed. (Boston: Joseph Bumstead, 1802), 97. My argument here has been influenced by Mark Seltzer's analysis of the deployment of gender in literary naturalism in his chapter "The Naturalist Machine," in *Bodies and Machines* (New York: Routledge, 1992), 23–43.

23 More, 104, 48.

24 In *White over Black: American Attitudes toward the Negro, 1550–1812* (Chapel Hill: University of North Carolina Press, 1968), Winthrop D. Jordan notes that early U.S. ethnographers frequently represented the Native American as "deficient in ardor and virility" (162). Cooper's contemporary Henry Lewis Morgan claimed that "the passion of love was entirely unknown among" the Iroquois. See Morgan's *League of the Iroquois* (1851; reprint New York: Corinth, 1962), 322.

25 My identification of Cora with the middle-class woman is complicated by the fact that, even though she has been raised white, she is in fact mulatta—the product of the British imperialist effort in the West Indies. It might be more accurate to say that Cora represents the Third World woman through whose agency the colonial power exerts its influence. In Frantz Fanon's analysis of "the colonialist program" in Algeria, "it was the woman who was given the historic mission of shaking up the Algerian man." One could argue that Cora performs a similar function for Uncas. Fanon's analysis appears in *A Dying Colonialism* (New York: Grove, 1965), 39 and is quoted in Kaplan, 673.

26 Renato Rosaldo, "Imperialist Nostalgia," in *Culture and Truth: The Remaking of Social Analysis* (Boston: Beacon Press, 1989), 70.

27 Kaplan, 664.

28 The classic statement of this position is, of course, Ann Douglas's *The Feminization of American Culture* (New York: Avon, 1977).

29 Richard H. Brodhead, *Cultures of Letters: Scenes of Reading and Writing in Nineteenth-Century America* (Chicago: University of Chicago Press, 1993), 41. Actually, this

characterization of maternal love appears in an antebellum publication entitled *Mother's Magazine* which Brodhead quotes; however, it is clear in context that Brodhead regards the quote as an accurate description of maternal authority.

30 Miller, 10; Douglas, 81.

31 Nancy Armstrong, *Desire and Domestic Fiction: A Political History of the Novel* (New York: Oxford University Press, 1987), 93; Christopher Lasch, *Haven in a Heartless World: The Family Besieged* (New York: Basic Books, 1977), 18.

32 I admit that "obliviousness" is probably too strong a word to use in Armstrong's case. On page 26 of the introduction to her book she manifests a good deal of self-consciousness about the gender politics of her own claims, even if she seems not to recognize the way in which they implicate her in the historical discourse she analyzes.

33 Previous feminist critiques of New Historicism include Judith Lowder Newton, "History as Usual? Feminism and the 'New Historicism,' " in *The New Historicism,* ed. H. Aram Veeser (New York: Routledge, 1989), 152–67, and Carolyn Porter, "Are We Being Historical Yet?" *South Atlantic Quarterly* 87 (fall 1988): 743–86.

Chapter 3   Black Nationalist Housekeeping: Maria W. Stewart

1 Maria W. Stewart, *Productions of Mrs. Maria W. Stewart* (1835), reprinted in the *Spiritual Narratives* volume of *The Schomburg Library of Nineteenth-Century Black Women Writers,* ed. Henry Louis Gates Jr. (New York: Oxford University Press, 1988), 59. The other modern edition of Stewart's work is edited by Marilyn Richardson and entitled *Maria W. Stewart: America's First Black Woman Political Writer, Essays and Speeches* (Bloomington: Indiana University Press, 1987). Richardson's edition is preferable for its annotation, its more thorough biographical and historical introduction, and its inclusion of the preface and autobiographical sketch which appeared in the 1879 edition of Stewart's works. Gates's edition, however, includes writings from Stewart's *Meditations* (Boston: Garrison and Knapp, 1832), omitted from Richardson. Readers desiring to acquaint themselves with all of Stewart's available writings will need to consult both editions. I am indebted to Richardson's book for introducing me to Stewart and for providing much of the contextual information and analytic groundwork for this chapter. Hereafter, quotations from Stewart will be taken from Gates's edition and cited parenthetically.

2 Examples include Valerie Smith, *Self-Discovery and Authority in Afro-American Narrative* (Cambridge, Mass.: Harvard University Press, 1987), 25–43; Richard Yarborough, "Race, Violence, and Manhood: The Masculine Ideal in Frederick Douglass's 'The Heroic Slave,' " *Frederick Douglass: New Literary and Historical Essays,* ed. Eric J. Sundquist (New York: Cambridge University Press, 1990), 166–88; and Eric J. Sundquist, *To Wake the Nations: Race in the Making of American Literature* (Cambridge, Mass.: Harvard University Press, 1993), 1–134. In *The Black Atlantic: Modernity and Double Consciousness* (Cambridge, Mass.: Harvard University Press, 1993), Paul Gilroy also discusses the interplay of gender and

nationalism in the Douglass / Covey scene. I engage Gilroy's reading in the final section of this chapter.

3 All of the scant biographical information available on Stewart is contained in Richardson's edition of Stewart's writings. Born Maria Miller in 1803, the orphaned Stewart grew up in service to a white minister's household in Connecticut. In 1826 she married a ship's outfitter who resided in Boston. Until 1829 Stewart enjoyed the comforts of a marriage to her relatively well-to-do husband James, but lawyers, apparently, defrauded her of the inheritance stipulated in his will (a fairly common means of confiscating the property of free blacks). After leaving Boston in 1834, Stewart (who was herself childless) dedicated the rest of her life to educating African American children in New York, Baltimore, and Washington, D.C. and, in this last city, worked as a matron in the Freedman's Hospital. She never remarried and sustained herself in low-paying teaching jobs or with the aid of church charity until 1878, when she was awarded a pension as a widow of a veteran of the War of 1812. Stewart died the following year. The exact nature of the criticism leading to Stewart's exile from Boston is unclear but probably grew at least in part out of disapproval of women lecturing on political topics. In *Free People of Color: Inside the African American Community* (Washington, D.C.: Smithsonian Institution Press, 1993), James Oliver Horton speculates that Stewart may have been forced to abandon her speaking career because she departed too far from gender conventions by "questioning [the] manhood" of audience members in her speech before the African Masonic Lodge in 1831 (109–10). Later in the chapter I complicate his reading somewhat by arguing that (in addition to whatever external encouragement she received) Stewart herself staged her eventual withdrawal from public life.

4 On the relationship between early black abolitionism and the later, more integrated abolitionist movement, see chapter 1 of Benjamin Quarles, *Black Abolitionists* (New York: Oxford University Press, 1969).

5 Sundquist, 123.

6 Sundquist, 92, 36, 34.

7 Sundquist himself argues for the necessity of a more thorough consideration of women nationalists (19).

8 Joyce Hope Scott points out in "From Foreground to Margin: Female Configuration and Masculine Self-Representation in Black Nationalist Fiction" (in *Nationalisms and Sexualities,* ed. Andrew Parker, Mary Russo, Doris Sommer, and Patricia Yaeger [New York: Routledge, 1992]) that other African American women took a position at the forefront of early black nationalism (even if they apparently did not lecture or publish). She cites their work in the late eighteenth century in benevolent and mutual aid societies and in abolitionist organizations that began forming the 1830s (298).

9 Stewart arrived in Boston in the same year that blacks established the Massachusetts General Colored Association, an abolitionist society and civil rights group. The following year, Samuel Cornish and John B. Russwurm, frustrated that whites had always "spoken for" blacks (often misrepresenting them in the

process), opened a Boston office of *Freedom's Journal,* the first African American newspaper. And one year later David Walker, in his "Address Delivered before the General Colored Association at Boston," declared the time had come for the "now enslaved children of Africa . . . to take their stand among the nations of the earth." Cornish and Russwurn's comment appears in an issue of *Freedom's Journal* dated 16 March 1827 and is reprinted in *Black Nationalism in America,* ed. John H. Bracey, August Meier, and Elliott Rudwick (Indianapolis and New York: Bobbs-Merrill, 1970), 24. David Walker's address appears in *Freedom's Journal,* 19 December 1828, and is reprinted in Bracey et. al, 29–34.

10 I am deducing this biographical trajectory from Stewart's elliptical comments on pages 40 to 42 of her "Meditation X," reprinted in Gates. For a far more detailed analysis of Stewart's relationship to both Christian doctrine and the church, see Carla L. Peterson's *Doers of the Word: African-American Women Speakers and Writers in the North (1830–1880)* (New York: Oxford University Press, 1995), 56–73.

11 Sterling Stuckey's *Slave Culture: Nationalist Theory and the Foundations of Black America* (New York: Oxford University Press, 1987) refers to Stewart in passing but describes her only as an "educator" (137). Stuckey's earlier collection, *The Ideological Origins of Black Nationalism* (Boston: Beacon Press, 1972), omits mention of Stewart altogether—as do *Black Nationalism in America,* edited by Bracey et al. and Wilson Jeremiah Moses's, *The Golden Age of Black Nationalism, 1850–1925* (New York: Oxford University Press, 1978). Stewart does make a brief appearance in Moses's later book, *The Wings of Ethiopia: Studies in African-American Life and Letters* (Ames: Iowa State University Press, 1990). There Moses writes that although Stewart "lacked the geopolitical ambitions of the true nationalist,"

> Nonetheless there was in her orations and meditations a nationalist spirit . . . and she clearly viewed black Americans as a nation, despite her lack of willingness to carry her nationalism to its ultimate logical expression of territorial separatism. (161)

The fact that Stewart, like many of the other nationalist writers discussed in *Golden Age,* did not advocate establishing a separate black homeland does not explain Moses's omission of her name from his earlier study. Nor does it explain why, when Moses does finally acknowledge Stewart, he feels compelled to insist upon territorial separatism as a definitional requirement for "true" nationalism.

12 See Sue E. Houchins's "Introduction" in Gates, xxix–xliv.

13 "Official" and "insurgent" are Alok Yadav's terms in his "Nationalism and Contemporaneity: Political Economy of a Discourse," *Cultural Critique* 26 (winter 1993–94): 191–229. Yadav uses "official" and "insurgent" to distinguish between two kinds of nationalism, the first "enforced from the top down, through the state apparatuses, repressive and ideological" and the second "directed against structures of domination, both intranational and international" (200). I will be describing early-nineteenth-century African American abolitionist and civil rights activism as "nationalist" in the latter sense of the term, although the concluding section of this chapter will complicate Yadav's distinction somewhat.

14   Cynthia Enloe, "Nationalism and Masculinity" in *Bananas, Beaches, and Bases: Making Feminist Sense of International Politics* (Berkeley and Los Angeles: University of California Press, 1989), 44.

15   Benedict Anderson, *Imagined Communities: Reflections on the Origin and Spread of Nationalism* (London: Verso, 1983), 12, as quoted in editors' introduction to Parker et al., 8.

16   Moses, *Golden Age*, 17.

17   Lawrence J. Friedman, *Gregarious Saints: Self and Community in American Abolitionism, 1830–1870* (New York: Cambridge University Press, 1982), 14; Quarles, 3–22.

18   Sermon by Peter Williams, quoted in Quarles, 7.

19   David Walker, *David Walker's Appeal, in Four Articles; Together with a Preamble, to the Coloured Citizens of the World,* ed. Charles M. Wiltse (New York: Hill and Wang, 1965), 55.

20   "Semi-mythical" refers to the archaic nature of the Ethiopia envisioned rather than to the question of its historic existence. For an evaluation of the truth-status of relevant depictions of ancient Ethiopia, see Martin Bernal, *Black Athena: The Afroasiatic Roots of Classical Civilization,* vol. 1 (New Brunswick, N.J.: Rutgers University Press, 1987). Moses defines Ethiopianism as a religious manifestation of black nationalism:

> The Ethiopian tradition derives from the Biblical verse, "Princes shall come out of Egypt; Ethiopia shall soon stretch forth her hands unto God." White abolitionists . . . had early sought to apply the verse to the situation of the black slave. Among black writers it made repeated appearances during the nineteenth century and by World War I, Ethiopianism had become not only a trans-Atlantic political movement, but a literary movement. . . . [It] involved a cyclical view of history—the idea that the ascendancy of the white race was only temporary, and that the divine providence of history was working to elevate the African peoples. (*Golden Age,* 23–4)

21   Despite the mysticism she shared with other early black nationalists and with later Pan-Africanists, Stewart's fabrication of a common identity for African Americans did not rely solely on what Moses calls the "racial chauvinism" of Ethiopianism (*Golden Age,* 23). No doubt Stewart sensed that conviction in common origins and mutual destiny alone could not overcome the seemingly monumental differences between the lives of free and enslaved blacks. Hence she used class as much as race to fabricate an African American identity. She writes, "Tell us no more of southern slavery; for with few exceptions . . . I consider our condition but little better than that." Free blacks, while not literally slaves, where nevertheless "confined by the chains of ignorance and poverty to lives of continual drudgery and toil" (51–3). According to chapter 5 of Leon F. Litwack's *North of Slavery: The Negro in the Free States, 1790–1860* (Chicago: University of Chicago Press, 1961) and chapter 2 of James Oliver Horton and Lois E. Horton's *Black Bostonians* (New York: Holmes and Meier, 1979), the vast majority

of free blacks in the Northern cities like Boston lived in poverty and depended upon menial employment for their survival; however, as Shirley Yee points out in *Black Women Abolitionists: A Study in Activism, 1828–1860* (Knoxville: University of Tennessee Press, 1992), many of the leaders of early black abolitionism came from "the few northern free black families that had amassed considerable wealth"—most notably, the Shadds, the Fortens, the Douglasses, the McCrummells, the Purvises, the Redmonds, the Chesters (12–6). Although Stewart was free-born and, in Yee's estimation, "enjoyed some measure of economic privilege and formal education" (113), her material circumstances were less exceptional than those of most of the other black women abolitionists Yee cites. Only a few years later, white middle-class women abolitionists like Sarah Grimké would insist that their status in a male-dominated society made them "slaves" too. Such acts of identification have received much criticism in contemporary scholarship, but the case of free blacks' identification with Southern slaves obviously requires a more complicated judgment (one which I will save for a more appropriate forum). Without impeaching the wisdom of Stewart's act of affiliation, I would nevertheless remark upon both its tendentiousness and novelty. Only by eliding the differences—first, between the lives of wealthy and working-class whites, and second, between those of free blacks and slaves—could Stewart achieve an African American first person plural.

22   Walker, 24–5.

23   Carole Pateman, *The Disorder of Women: Democracy, Feminism and Political Theory* (Stanford, Calif.: Stanford University Press, 1989), 43–5. The sexual depredations committed against women by the institution of slavery gave Walker's distrust a particular cultural inflection, of course; sexual chattelism and miscegenation made the slave woman's sentimental weakness open to construction as sexual vulnerability—or even sexual pliability. Any sexual subtext conveyed in the anecdote, however, would only augment its already manifest skepticism about women's reliability.

24   Pateman (paraphrasing a comment made by Enoch Powell to the British House of Commons in 1981), 50.

25   Douglass's editorial appeared in the 2 March 1863 edition of *Douglass' Paper* and is quoted in Ronald T. Takaki, *Violence in the Black Imagination: Essays and Documents* (New York: G. P. Putnam's and Sons, 1972), 24. Also see chapter 4 of Horton's *Free People* for more on attitudes towards political violence in the black abolitionist movement.

26   Benedict Anderson, *Imagined Communities: Reflections on the Origin and Spread of Nationalism,* rev. ed. (New York: Verso, 1991), 7.

27   On Walker's death see Wiltse's Introduction to Walker's *Appeal,* xi. Stewart refers to Walker's assassination in the introduction to her speeches (5).

28   See, for example, Stewart, 20. Ronald T. Takaki describes Douglass's ambivalence toward violence on 17–33 of his book.

29   R. Radhakrishnan, "Nationalism, Gender, and the Narrative of Identity" in Parker et al., 78.

30 Enloe, 61.

31 Frederick Douglass, lecture delivered before the Rochester Ladies' Anti-Slavery Society, Jan. 1855; reprinted in Philip Foner, ed., *The Life and Writings of Frederick Douglass,* vol. 2 (New York: International, 1950), 349–50, and quoted in Yee, 147.

32 Enloe, 62.

33 Eileen Boris, "The Power of Motherhood: Black and White Activist Women Redefine the 'Political' " in *Mothers of a New World: Maternalist Politics and the Origins of Welfare States,* ed. Seth Koven and Sonya Michel (New York: Routledge, 1993), 213–4.

34 Richardson, 9–10.

35 Horton contends that although black women in the antebellum North were "encouraged to take on reform activities that departed from the gender expectations in the wider society and that although black men were generally supportive of these reform efforts," the free black community also "accepted many conventional notions about women's sphere" (*Free People,* 109, 117).

36 Catharine E. Beecher, *A Treatise on Domestic Economy* (Boston, 1842), 36–7; quoted in Sacvan Bercovitch, *The Rites of Assent: Transformations in the Symbolic Construction of America* (New York: Routledge University Press, 1993), 189.

37 Gilroy, 64, 68.

38 Ibid., 68.

39 Cf. Homi K. Bhabha's discussion of the split temporality of nationalist narratives in his essay, "DissemiNation: Time, Narrative, and the Margins of the Modern Nation" in *Nation and Narration,* ed. Homi K. Bhabha (New York: Routledge, 1990), 291–322.

40 Frederick Douglass, *Life and Times of Frederick Douglass* (New York: Collier, 1962), 473–4; quoted in Takaki, 32.

41 Claudia Tate, *Domestic Allegories of Political Desire: The Black Heroine's Text at the Turn of the Century* (New York: Oxford University Press, 1992), 5.

42 Houston A. Baker, Jr., *Workings of the Spirit: The Poetics of Afro-American Women's Writing* (Chicago: University of Chicago Press, 1991), 32–3.

Chapter 4   Bio-Political Resistance: Harriet Beecher Stowe

1 Particularly compelling examples of such work include Richard Yarborough "Strategies of Black Characterization in *Uncle Tom's Cabin* and the Early Afro-American Novel," in *New Essays on* Uncle Tom's Cabin, ed. Eric J. Sundquist (New York: Cambridge University Press, 1986), 45–84; Hortense J. Spillers, "Changing the Letter: The Yokes, the Jokes of Discourse, or, Mrs. Stowe, Mr. Reed," in *Slavery and the Literary Imagination,* ed. Deborah E. McDowell and Arnold Rampersad (Baltimore, Md.: Johns Hopkins University Press, 1989), 25–61; Harryette Mullen, "Runaway Tongue: Resistant Orality in *Uncle Tom's Cabin, Our Nig, Incidents in the Life of a Slave Girl,* and *Beloved,*" in *The Culture of Sentiment: Race, Gender, and Sentimentality in 19th Century America,* ed. Shirley

Samuels (New York: Oxford University Press, 1992), 244–64; James Baldwin, "Everybody's Protest Novel," reprinted in *Notes of a Native Son* (New York: Bantam, 1955), 9–17; and chapter 7 of Leon F. Litwack's *North of Slavery: The Negro in the Free States, 1790–1860* (Chicago: University of Chicago Press, 1961), 214–46.

2   For a more detailed discussion of the political problematics of white women abolitionists' identification with slaves, see Karen Sánchez-Eppler, *Touching Liberty: Abolition, Feminism, and the Politics of the Body* (Berkeley and Los Angeles: University of California Press, 1993).

3   For more on Stowe's illness, see Forrest Wilson, *Crusader in Crinoline: The Life of Harriet Beecher Stowe* (Philadelphia: J. B. Lippincott, 1941), and Joan D. Hedrick, *Harriet Beecher Stowe: A Life* (New York: Oxford University Press, 1994), esp. 173–85. On Dr. Wesselheoft's Hydropathic Institute, see Howard R. Kemble and Harry B. Weiss, *The Great American Watercure Craze: A History of Hydropathy in the United States* (Trenton, N.J.: Past Times, 1967), 209–18. For more on Beecher's relation to the watercure, see Kathryn Kish Sklar, *Catharine Beecher: A Study in American Domesticity* (New York: Norton, 1976), 204–9.

4   Previous discussions of Stowe's relation to her sister's domestic ideology to which I am indebted are: Elizabeth Ammons, "Stowe's Dream of the Mother-Savior: *Uncle Tom's Cabin* and American Women Writers before the 1920s," in Sundquist, 155–95; Richard H. Brodhead, *Cultures of Letters: Scenes of Reading and Writing in Nineteenth-Century America* (Chicago: University of Chicago Press, 1993), 13–47; Jane Tompkins, *Sensational Designs: The Cultural Work of American Fiction, 1790–1860* (New York: Oxford University Press, 1985), 122–46; Philip Fisher, *Hard Facts: Setting and Form in the American Novel* (New York: Oxford University Press, 1985), 87–127; Glenna Matthews, *"Just a Housewife": The Rise and Fall of Domesticity in America* (New York: Oxford University Press, 1987), 35–65; Laurie Crumpacker, "Four Novels of Harriet Beecher Stowe: A Study of Nineteenth-Century Androgyny," in *American Novelists Revisited: Essays in Feminist Criticism*, ed. Fritz Fleischmann (Boston: G. K. Hall, 1982), 78–106; and Jeanne Boydston, Mary Kelley, and Ann Margolis, *The Limits of Sisterhood: The Beecher Sisters on Women's Rights and Woman's Sphere* (Chapel Hill: University of North Carolina Press, 1988).

5   Foucault writes that bio-power takes on issues such as "the problems of birthrate, longevity, public health, housing, and migration" (*The History of Sexuality: An Introduction*, trans. Robert Hurley [New York: Vintage, 1980], 140) and that "its aim is to strengthen the social forces—to increase production, to develop the economy, spread education, raise the level of public morality; to increase and multiply" (*Discipline and Punish: The Birth of the Prison*, trans. Alan Sheridan [New York: Vintage Books, 1979], 208).

6   Jacques Donzelot, *The Policing of Families*, trans. Robert Hurley (New York: Pantheon, 1979), 6–7.

7   Michel Foucault, "Body/Power," trans. Colin Gordon et al., in *Power/Knowledge: Selected Interviews and Other Writings, 1972–1977*, ed. Colin Gordon (New York:

Oxford University Press, 1980), 55. Although evidence suggests that there may have been a physiological basis for Stowe's infirmity, that does not mean that her "hysteria" is exempt from cultural, ideological, or institutional analysis (see note 10 below).

8   Tompkins, 144. For other examples of feminist oppositional readings of Stowe and domesticity, see Elizabeth Ammons, "Heroines in *Uncle Tom's Cabin*," in *Critical Essays on Harriet Beecher Stowe*, ed. Elizabeth Ammons (Boston: G. K. Hall, 1980), 153, and Nina Baym, *Novels, Readers, and Reviewers: Responses to Fiction in Antebellum America* (Ithaca, N.Y.: Cornell University Press, 1984), 189.

9   Foucault, *History of Sexuality*, 93–6.

10   Quoted in Charles Stowe, *Life and Letters of Harriet Beecher Stowe* (Boston and New York: Houghton, Mifflin, 1889), 111, 101. Hedrick speculates that Stowe's apparently "hysterical" symptoms may in fact have been the result of chronic mercury poisoning caused by the drug calomel, a blue pill routinely prescribed by allopathic physicians in the 1830s and 1840s for a multitude of diseases. In addition to "headache or 'neuralgia,' loss of control of the hands, lassitude, . . . mental disorganization," mercury poisoning, may also result in both "a blurring of vision" and "gross constriction of visual fields" (Hedrick, 174–5 and 431, n. 10). These last two symptoms (suggesting, as they seem to do, both an inability to focus visually and an excess of focus) help account for Stowe's specific articulation of her illness, and I cite them to add credence to my thesis that, for Stowe, the abstruse categories of absorption and abstraction were intimately related to her representation (and indeed her experience) of the body. Of course, the possible physiological basis of her illness cannot by itself account for Stowe's interpretation of the meaning of her symptoms, and, conversely, the meaning that she, through the help of domesticity's womanist values, attached to her symptoms no doubt altered her sensational experience of them.

11   Quoted in Charles Stowe, 92; quoted in Edward Wagenknecht, *Harriet Beecher Stowe: The Known and the Unknown* (New York: Oxford University Press, 1965), 54; quoted in Charles Stowe, 115, 92.

12   Catharine E. Beecher, *Letters to the People on Health and Happiness* (New York: Harper and Brothers, 1855), 111, 105.

13   Catharine E. Beecher, *Treatise on Domestic Economy* (1841; reprint New York: Schocken Books, 1977), 148.

14   Cf. G. J. Barker-Benfield's discussion of what he interprets as the inherently misogynist concept of bodily economy in *The Horrors of the Half-Known Life: Male Attitudes toward Women and Sexuality in Nineteenth-Century America* (New York: Harper and Row, 1976), and William Leach's statement in *True Love and Perfect Union: The Feminist Reform of Sex and Society* (New York: Basic Books, 1980), that the concept of bodily economy served the interests of "an emerging hierarchical corporate capitalist system dominated by men" (351).

15   On the reform of female education in this period, see Nancy F. Cott, *The Bonds of Womanhood: "Woman's Sphere" in New England, 1780–1835* (New Haven, Conn.: Yale University Press, 1977), 101–25; Linda K. Kerber, *Women of the Republic:*

Intellect and Ideology in Revolutionary America (Chapel Hill: University of North Carolina Press, 1980), 185–231; Sklar, 75–6; Donzelot, 39; and Armstrong, 59–95.

16   Beecher, *Treatise,* 144, 18, 149, 144–5, 147.

17   Harriet Beecher Stowe, "Irritability," from *Little Foxes* in *Stories, Sketches and Studies* (New York: AMS Press, 1967), 357.

18   Hannah More, *Strictures on the Modern System of Female Education,* 3rd American ed. (Boston: Joseph Bumstead, 1802), 40.

19   Carroll Smith-Rosenberg, "The Hysterical Woman: Sex Roles and Role Conflict in Nineteenth-Century America," in *Disorderly Conduct: Visions of Gender in Victorian America* (New York: Oxford University Press, 1985), 205.

20   Donzelot, xxii.

21   Smith-Rosenberg, 205.

22   Armstrong, 80.

23   Donzelot, 9.

24   In prefatory comments to her chapter on Hawthorne's *The House of the Seven Gables,* Gillian Brown makes similar connections between Beecher's call for a more "systematic" household and Stowe's representation of the division of labor effected by slavery, and she also links both to Donzelot's work. The burden of proof of originality, however, falls upon Brown rather than myself; the article on which my chapter is based was published before the appearance of Brown's book. Moreover, Brown does not reference that article. Compare Brown's *Domestic Individualism: Imagining Self in Nineteenth-Century America* (Berkeley and Los Angeles: University of California Press, 1990), 63–9, with my article, "Bio-Political Resistance and Domestic Ideology," *American Literary History* I (winter 1989): esp. 717–20 and 722–25.

25   Harriet Beecher Stowe, *Uncle Tom's Cabin; or, Life Among the Lowly,* 2 vols. (Boston: J. P. Jewett, 1852), vol. 2, 21. Future quotations from Stowe's novel will be taken from this edition and cited parenthetically.

26   Henry Hughes, *Treatise on Sociology* (1854; reprint New York Negro Universities Press, 1968), 86.

27   William A. Alcott, *Lectures on Life and Health* (Boston: Phillips, Sampson, and Company, 1853), 273.

28   James Clark, *The Sanative Influence of Climate* (Philadelphia: A. Waldie, 1841), 31; Alcott, 269.

29   Stowe, *Stories,* 354.

30   I realize that my interpretation of Little Eva's illness and death goes against critical consensus, which has represented Eva's consumption in positive terms, as part and parcel of the larger transcendence of "the physical" necessitated by evangelical belief that "it is the spirit alone that is finally real" (see Tompkins, 133). But Stowe's Christianity was of a more muscular variety than critics have generally assumed. In an article appearing in her "The Chimney-Corner" series, Stowe actually attacked revivals of religion because they so "often end in periods of bodily ill-health." Stowe states in this article that the body need *not* be

transcended by the true believer. In fact, "The body, if allowed the slightest degree of fair play, so far from being a contumacious infidel and opposer, becomes a very fair Christian helper, and, instead of throttling the soul, gives it wings to rise to celestial regions." See Stowe's "Bodily Religion: A Sermon on Good Health," *Atlantic Monthly* 18 (Jan. 1866): 90. Hedrick reports that in the mid-1840s, Stowe urged her minister husband to "preach a sermon on the relationship between bodily health and religion" (178).

31 Stowe, *Stories,* 359.

32 Catharine E. Beecher, *An Essay on Slavery and Abolitionism* (1837; reprint Freeport, N.Y.: Books for Libraries, 1970), 94, 21.

33 Foucault, *The History of Sexuality,* 96.

34 D. A. Miller, "*Cage aux folles:* Sensation and Gender in Wilkie Collins's *The Woman in White,*" in *The Novel and the Police* (Berkeley and Los Angeles: University of California Press, 1988), 148.

35 For a provocative analysis of Stowe's animism, see Lynn Wardley, "Relic, Fetish, Femmage: The Aesthetics of Sentiment in the Work of Stowe," *Yale Journal of Criticism* 5 (1992): 165–91 and reprinted in Samuels, 203–220.

36 Harriet Beecher Stowe, *A Key to Uncle Tom's Cabin* (New York: AMS, 1967), 394.

37 Miller, 122; Brodhead, 28.

38 Foucault, *Power / Knowledge,* 58.

39 Foucault, *Discipline and Punish,* 194.

40 Michel Foucault, "The Ethic of Care for the Self as a Practice of Freedom: An Interview," trans. J. D. Gauthier, in *The Final Foucault,* ed. James Bernauer and David Rasmussen (Cambridge, Mass.: MIT Press, 1988), 11.

41 Judith Butler, "Variations on Sex and Gender: Beauvoir, Wittig and Foucault," in *Feminism as Critique: On the Politics of Gender,* ed. Seyla Benhabib and Drucilla Cornell (Minneapolis: University of Minnesota Press, 1987), 128.

Chapter 5 *Homosocial Romance: Nathaniel Hawthorne*

1 Nathaniel Hawthorne, *The Scarlet Letter,* vol. I of *The Centenary Edition of the Works of Nathaniel Hawthorne* (Columbus: Ohio State University Press, 1962), 140. Subsequent quotations from *The Scarlet Letter* will be taken from this edition and cited parenthetically.

2 Eve Kosofsky Sedgwick, *Between Men: English Literature and Male Homosocial Desire* (New York: Columbia University Press, 1985), 91.

3 Nathaniel Hawthorne, *The American Notebooks,* vol. VIII of *The Centenary Edition of the Works of Nathaniel Hawthorne* (Columbus: Ohio State University Press, 1972), 183. Subsequent quotations from Hawthorne's notebooks will be taken from this edition and cited parenthetically.

4 Robert Penn Warren, "Hawthorne Revisited: Some Remarks on Hellfiredness," *The Sewanee Review* 81 (Jan.–Mar. 1973): 107. Scott S. Derrick offered a very persuasive reading of Hawthorne's Chillingworth-Dimmesdale plot within the context of Sedgwick's homosocial / homoerotic triangle in his paper, "Homo-

phobia, Homosociality, and Authorship in *The Scarlet Letter*" (presented at the American Literature Association's Annual Conference on American Literature, Baltimore, Md., 28 May 1993).

5   Sedgwick, 21.

6   In "*The Scarlet Letter* as a Love Story" (*PMLA* 4 [Sept. 1962]: 425–35), Ernest Sandeen describes Hawthorne's work as "the typical love story of our Western tradition" inasmuch as the plot is based on an erotic triangle.

7   One exception is critic Monika Elbert, who argues at some length for the homoerotic nature of the relationship between Chillingworth and Dimmesdale. Elbert, noting as I have, that "there is something sexual in Chillingworth's search for mastery over Dimmesdale," contends that Dimmesdale reciprocates the passion. See Elbert's "Hester on the Scaffold, Dimmesdale in the Closet: Hawthorne's Seven-Year Itch," *Essays in Literature* 16 (fall 1989): 234–55. Also see Robert K. Martin, "Hester Pyrnne *C'est Moi*: Nathaniel Hawthorne and the Anxieties of Gender," in *Engendering Men,* ed. Joseph Boone and Michael Cadden (New York: Routledge, 1990), 122–39. For a compelling rationale for *not* reading the Chillingworth-Dimmesdale plot in homoerotic terms, see Christopher Newfield, "The Politics of Male Suffering: Masochism and Hegemony in the American Renaissance," *differences* 1, no. 3 (1989): 79, n. 8.

8   Biographer Edwin Haviland Miller upsets this image of Hawthorne somewhat by emphasizing the intensity of Hawthorne's friendships with men. For Miller, Melville's apparent infatuation with Hawthorne was just one in a series of equivocal male friendships punctuating Hawthorne's adult life. See Miller, *Salem Is My Dwelling Place: A Life of Nathaniel Hawthorne* (Iowa City: University of Iowa Press, 1991), 70–1; 192–95; 217–22; 299–318.

9   Henry James, "Hawthorne," in *The Shock of Recognition,* ed. Edmund Wilson (1879; reprint New York: Modern Library, 1943), 565.

10 Richard H. Brodhead, *The School of Hawthorne* (New York: Oxford University Press, 1986), 48. In his study of Hawthorne's relation to domesticity, *Dearest Beloved: The Hawthornes and the Making of the Middle-Class Family* (Berkeley and Los Angeles: University of California Press, 1993), T. Walter Herbert describes the tensions in the Hawthorne family that such images of their domestic felicity conceal.

11 I admit that, in the end, it is impossible to distinguish between "personal" sexual preferences and "social" conditions for interpersonal relationships. I make the distinction between sexual and social here only to differentiate my project from a more traditional biographical interpretation that would read the Dimmesdale-Chillingworth plot as symptomatic of Hawthorne's own repressed homosexuality.

12 Sedgwick, 1, 89.

13 Evan Carton, *The Rhetoric of American Romance: Dialectic and Identity in Emerson, Dickinson, Poe, and Hawthorne* (Baltimore, Md.: Johns Hopkins University Press, 1985), 207, 209.

14   David Leverenz, *Manhood and the American Renaissance* (Ithaca, N.Y.: Cornell University Press, 1989), 2, 16.

15   John McWilliams, "The Rationale for 'The American Romance,' " *boundary 2* 17 (1990): 72.

16   See Nina Baym, "Melodramas of Beset Manhood: How Theories of American Literature Exclude Women," in her *Feminism & American Literary History: Essays* (New Brunswick, N.J.: Rutgers University Press, 1992), 3–18.

17   Leverenz, 17–8.

18   Leverenz mentions his intellectual debt to feminist criticism and theory on p. 2.

19   In "The Traffic in Women," Gayle Rubin defines a "sex / gender system" as a "set of arrangements by which a society transforms biological sexuality into products of human activity." Rubin's article appears in *Toward an Anthropology of Women,* ed. Reyna R. Reiter (New York: Monthly Review Press, 1975), 159. Also see Rubin's further commentary on the term in her "Thinking Sex: Notes Towards a Radical Theory of the Politics of Sexuality," in *Pleasure and Danger: Exploring Female Sexuality,* ed. Carole S. Vance (Boston: Routledge and Kegan Paul, 1984), 307ff.

20   Miller provides a thorough account of the friendship between Hawthorne and Horatio Bridge. See pages 100–1 for his description of Hawthorne's visit. Also see Bridge's recollections of the summer in Augusta in his *Personal Recollections of Nathaniel Hawthorne* (New York: Harper and Brothers Publishers, 1893), 63–7.

21   I believe it is important to resist the heterosexual developmental narrative that might tempt us to dismiss the significance of Hawthorne's living arrangements by reference to his sexual "immaturity." Furthermore, the fact that Hawthorne presents his paradise of bachelors as a temporary interlude does not make his residence in Augusta any less sexually equivocal. As Jeff Nunokawa explains in " 'All the Sad Young Men': AIDS and the Work of Mourning," when men who love other men can be represented at all, it is often in the elegiac mode appropriate to the heterosexual developmental narrative which makes homosexuality into an immature sexual phase. Nunokawa's essay appears in *Inside / Out: Lesbian Theories, Gay Theories,* ed. Diana Fuss (New York: Routledge, 1991), 311–23.

22   See Bridge, 63, 66.

23   Miller, 100.

24   Hawthorne credits Schaeffer with the name's invention on page 46 of *The American Notebooks.*

25   Eve Kosofsky Sedgwick, *Epistemology of the Closet* (Berkeley and Los Angeles: University of California Press, 1990), 187, 131–80.

26   Martin, 130.

27   Quoted in Herbert, 4.

28   Ibid., 174–5.

29   Catharine E. Beecher, *Treatise on Domestic Economy* (1841; reprint New York: Schocken Books, 1977), 144–8. See chapter 4 for a more detailed discussion of Beecher along these lines.

30   Lauren Berlant, *The Anatomy of National Fantasy: Hawthorne, Utopia, and Everyday Life* (Chicago: University of Chicago Press, 1991), 191.

31   Ibid., 192.

32   Martin, 130.

33   Nathaniel Hawthorne, "Wakefield," in *Twice-Told Tales,* vol. ix of *The Centenary Edition of the Works of Nathaniel Hawthorne* (Columbus: Ohio State University Press, 1974), 133, 138.

34   The drowning is, of course, thought to be the model for Zenobia's death in *The Blithedale Romance.*

35   George Dekker, "Once More: Hawthorne and the Genealogy of American Romance," *ESQ* 35 (1989): 71. Dekker cites an entry in the 1828 edition of Webster's *An American Dictionary of the English Language.* "Romance," it reads, "differs from the novel, as it treats great actions and extraordinary adventures, that is, . . . it vaults or soars beyond the limits of fact and real life, and often of probability."

36   Brodhead, 3–47.

37   This section of "The Custom-House" is, evidently, based on an entry appearing on pages 283–4 of *The American Notebooks.* Hawthorne's description of himself "peeping" (quoted above) concludes his description of the room in the notebook version.

38   Naomi Schor, *Reading in Detail: Aesthetics and the Feminine* (New York: Routledge, 1987), 4.

39   Andreas Huyssen, *After the Great Divide: Modernism, Mass Culture, Postmodernism* (Bloomington and Indianapolis: Indiana University Press, 1986), 47.

40   Letter to William D. Ticknor (17 Feb. 1854), printed in *The Letters, 1853–56,* vol. XVII of *The Centenary Edition of the Works of Nathaniel Hawthorne* (Columbus: Ohio State University Press, 1987), 177.

41   Letter to Ticknor (24 April 1857), printed in *Letters of Hawthorne to William D. Ticknor: 1851–1864* (Washington, D.C.: NCR / Microcard Editions, 1972), 50.

42   Letter to Ticknor (5 February 1855), printed in *The Letters, 1853–56,* 308.

43   Hawthorne, preface to *The Snow-Image,* in *The Snow-Image and Uncollected Tales,* vol. XI of *The Centenary Edition of the Works of Nathaniel Hawthorne* (Columbus: Ohio State University Press, 1974), 4.

44   Hawthorne, "The Old Manse," in *Mosses From an Old Manse,* vol. X of *The Centenary Edition of the Works of Nathaniel Hawthorne* (Columbus: Ohio State University Press, 1974), 33.

45   Quoted in Gordon Hutner, *Secrets and Sympathy: Forms of Disclosure in Hawthorne's Novels* (Athens: University of Georgia Press, 1988), 7.

46   Deborah Masden, "The Romance of the New World," *Journal of American Studies* 24 (1990): 104.

47   Gerald Graff, "American Criticism Left and Right," in *Ideology and Classic American Literature,* ed. Sacvan Bercovitch and Myra Jehlen (New York: Cambridge University Press, 1986), 112–3. For a more sustained consideration of the politics of self-reflexive art in contemporary criticism, see my article, " 'When

Something Goes Queer': Familiarity, Formalism, and Minority Intellectuals in the 1980s," *Yale Journal of Criticism* 6 (spring 1993): 121–41.

Conclusion

1 Robert K. Martin, "Hester Prynne *C'est Moi:* Nathaniel Hawthorne and the Anxieties of Gender," in *Engendering Men,* ed. Joseph Boone and Michael Cadden (New York: Routledge, 1990), 130. According to Martin, "Hawthorne's art represents a world in which no meanings are fixed, in which everything is always a polysemous surface awaiting interpretation." Martin emphasizes the disruptive consequence this has on male identity in *The Scarlet Letter,* in which he detects "a refusal of the gender boundaries instilled in everyday life, the habits and customs that have overridden the ambiguities of nature" (128). Hawthorne could challenge conventional gender boundaries because he, as a practitioner of the "unmanly" art of writing, did not feel entirely at home in his profession (122). Martin's essay, however, also counters more utopian readings by stressing the anxiety indeterminacy provoked in Hawthorne. Nevertheless, I believe it is appropriate to place the essay in the tradition of criticism I am describing; even if he suggests that Hawthorne did not entirely fulfill the subversive potential of his premodernist aesthetics, Martin still uses the "feminization" of culture as a means of asserting the male writer's unique access to a subversive aesthetics.

2 Andreas Huyssen, *After the Great Divide: Modernism, Mass Culture, Postmodernism* (Bloomington and Indianapolis: Indiana University Press, 1986), 47.

3 Michel Foucault, *The History of Sexuality: An Introduction,* trans. Robert Hurley (New York: Vintage, 1985), 100–1.

4 Ibid., 85.

5 Ibid., 94.

❧ INDEX

Scarlet Letter, The: alienated men and, 93–94, 100, 103–105; defamiliarization of domestic in, 98–99, 101, 103; feminization of society, 16–17; gothic in, 89, 99; Hester as rebel, 99–100; homophobia generated by, 92, 104, 106; homosocial/homoerotic continuum, 90–91, 106, 134 n.11; and modernist canon, 91–93, 97, 102–105; paranoia, Dimmesdale's, 89; perspectival shifts, 92, 105; realism as feminine, 93, 99, 100–102; refamiliarization of Hester, 100; romance as masculine, 101–103, 136 n.35; sex/gender system and self-reflexive text, 94, 104, 106. *See also* Hawthorne, Nathaniel

Schaeffer, M., 94–96

Schor, Naomi, 102

Scott, Joyce Hope, 29, 125 n.8

Sedgwick, Catharine Maria: *Hope Leslie,* 26

Sedgwick, Eve Kosofsky, 89–92, 96–97

Sigourney, Lydia: *Letters to Mothers,* 31

Slavery, 9, 21. *See also Productions of Mrs. Maria W. Stewart; Uncle Tom's Cabin*

Smith, Elizabeth Oakes: *Woman and Her Needs,* 30, 118 n.20

Smith-Rosenberg, Carroll, 77

Social, the, 33–34

Stewart, Maria W.: biographical background, 53–54, 67, 125 n.3; Boston as context for activism, 125 n.9, 129 n.35. *See also Productions of Mrs. Maria W. Stewart*

Stowe, Harriet Beecher: Catharine Beecher's influence on, 74–77; Civil War, view of, 24; hysteria, experience of, 71–72, 73–74, 76, 130 nn.7 and 10; stimulants, opinion of, 76, 80. *See also Key to Uncle Tom's Cabin, A; Minister's Wooing, The; Oldtown Folks; Pearl of Orr's Island, The; Uncle Tom's Cabin*

Studley, Mary: *What Our Girls Ought to Know,* 32

Sundquist, Eric J., 52–55, 61, 66

Tate, Claudia, 27–29, 65, 67

Thoreau, Henry David: *Walden,* 44–45

Tompkins, Jane, 2, 19, 72

Truth, Sojourner: *Narrative of Sojourner Truth,* 28–29

Uncle Tom's Cabin: abolitionism and biopolitics in, 70–71, 78–79, 81–82, 86–87; African Americans, representation of, 70–71, 78, 80–81, 83–84; class, representation of, 76, 78–81; housekeeping in, 80–81; consumption of body in, 79–80; and education of women, 71, 75–77, 79; Eva's death, 22, 79, 132 n.30; and feminist criticism, 72–73; and Foucauldian criticism, 82–83, 86–87; and gender difference, 71; hysteria, impact of Stowe's on, 78–81; mass culture, 71, 87–88; nervous characters in, 71, 78–80; patriarchy, as critique of, 71, 77, 110; power vs. resistance in, 71–73, 83, 86–88; powerlessness in, 70–71, 83, 86, 88; slave labor, 78, 80–81; subjectivity (selfhood) and, 71, 77–78, 81–87. *See also* Stowe, Harriet Beecher

"Wakefield": self-reflexivity in, 99. *See also* Hawthorne, Nathaniel

Walker, David, 53, 54; *David Walker's Appeal,* 57, 58–59, 60

Wexler, Laura, 3

White, Barbara A., 13

Wilson, Harriet E.: *Our Nig,* 27–28

Women writers. *See* Domestic fiction; Domesticity; *individual authors and works*

Lora Romero is Assistant Professor of English at Stanford
University.

Library of Congress Cataloging-in-Publication Data
Romero, Lora.
Home fronts : domesticity and its critics in the Antebellum United
States / by Lora Romero.
p.   cm. — (New Americanists)
Includes bibliographical references and index.
ISBN 0-8223-2030-4 (alk. paper). — ISBN 0-8223-2042-8 (alk.
paper)
1. American fiction—19th century—History and criticism.
2. Domestic fiction, American—History and criticism. 3. Cooper,
James Fenimore, 1789–1851—Political and social views.
4. Stowe, Harriet Beecher, 1811–1896—Political and social
views.   5. Hawthorne, Nathaniel, 1804–1864—Political and
social views.   6. Stewart, Maria W., 1803–1879—Political and
social views.   7. Literature and society—United States—
History—19th century.   8. Women and literature—United
States—History—19th century.   9. Home—United States—
History—19th century—Historiography.   10. Authorship—Sex
differences. I. Title. II. Series.
PS374.D57R64   1997
813'.309355—dc21   97-7611   CIP